THE DUKE OF PALERMO

BOOKS BY EDMUND WILSON

THE DUKE OF PALERMO

and Other Plays,

with an Open Letter to Mike Nichols

EDMUND WILSON

FARRAR, STRAUS AND GIROUX
NEW YORK

Copyright © 1930, 1967, 1969 by Edmund Wilson
Library of Congress catalog card number: 69-13734
All rights reserved
Published simultaneously in Canada by
Doubleday Canada Ltd., Toronto
Printed in the United States of America

ACKNOWLEDGMENTS

The Duke of Palermo and the *Open Letter to Mike Nichols* first appeared in the *New York Review of Books, Dr. McGrath* in *Commentary*, and the second scene of *Osbert's Career* in the *New Republic*.

I am indebted to Mr. Ira Mendlowitz for composing the Elizabethan song.

CONTENTS

The Lamentable Tragedy of

THE DUKE OF PALERMO

1966

SCENE I

Professor Winslow's living room at Hillsdale, a small New England college. A door at stage right of the back wall leads to the central hallway and the front door, and a door in the side wall at stage left leads to the Professor's study, into which, though we do not see it, another door from the corridor gives access. The door into the hall is open. A fireplace in the center of the back wall. The room has been furnished in very good taste by the late Mrs. Winslow, a portrait of whom as a young girl hangs over the fireplace. On the table, in a silver frame, is a large photograph of her. The Professor's nineteen-year-old daughter Fran is lounging in an arm-chair reading Mad *magazine, with one shoe dangling from her toe. Chuck Chambers, a young instructor, enters from the door to the corridor. He looks more like a student than an instructor: corduroys, sneakers, a jersey, a bristling crew haircut.*

FRAN (*looking up but not rising or changing her position*). Why didn't you ring?

CHUCK. Your father's always glad to see me.

FRAN. How do you know *I* am?

CHUCK. That doesn't influence me. (*Handing her*

a copy of Liberation.) If you can tear yourself away from that garbage, you might care to look at this. It's got a firsthand account of Alabama. I suppose we ought to have gone.

FRAN (*taking the magazine*). I see you've stopped cleaning your nails?

CHUCK. They'd just get dirty again.

FRAN. You've got more blackheads around your nose. You're the most disgusting object on the campus.

CHUCK. That's why I haven't been around lately. I didn't want to disgust you. Do you think I'm more disgusting than Spooky Simms?

FRAN. He at least wears a clean shirt.

CHUCK. Is that why you see so much of him?

FRAN. I don't.

CHUCK. You went to the Middlebury game with him.

FRAN. I don't want to get him against me. He's trying to downgrade Father.

CHUCK. How can he? Your father's got life tenure.

FRAN. They want him to teach Freshmen courses and give up his regular lectures.

CHUCK. Your father's an institution. He's been giving that Shakespeare course for years.

FRAN. But Spooky is the head of the department, and he can dictate to most of the others.

CHUCK. I suppose they can't stand having your father putting on such a successful show and divert-

ing attention from their goddam explications. I
know that they think he's a ham, and so in a way
he is. But I can't help respecting the old boy. Your
father doesn't give a damn about how much of a
fool he makes of himself so long as he can put over
good literature. When he used to give us Shelley's
Skylark, he'd flap his arms like this so you'd expect
him to soar off the platform. (*He demonstrates.*)
            "Hail to thee, blithe Spirit!
            Bird thou never wert" . . .
He'd act out every character in Shakespeare from
Iago to Sir Toby Belch. As Ophelia, he was abso-
lutely priceless. When he read that last poem of
Browning's about greeting the Unseen with a cheer,
half the class gave the Hillsdale yell.

FRAN. That never happened.

CHUCK. They also say he used to do a morris
dance with bells on his ankles.

FRAN. That's another legend.

CHUCK. It's finding that unknown Elizabethan
play that's made them all furious. You think it's
genuine?

FRAN. He thinks so.

CHUCK. Were you with him when he found it?

FRAN. No. I was staying in London. He was off
on a hike by himself.

CHUCK. Why hasn't he shown it to anybody?

FRAN. He wants to edit it himself—and he wants
to have it acted first.

CHUCK. Of course: he wants to wow them. He's playing the Duke, I understand. Well, if it *is* authentic, they'll never forgive him; and if it isn't, they can say he's nuts. It's a pity that the first production has to depend on the talents of Hillsdale!

Professor Winslow enters stage right. Bone spectacles, an old-fashioned Van Dyck beard, a green velvet waistcoat and an orange silk necktie secured by a ring. He is radiant; at fifty-four, still full of almost boyish enthusiasm.

WINSLOW. Well, I think I've made out a good case!

CHUCK. You mean about the authorship?

WINSLOW. I think there can be no doubt that the play is by Henry Chettle! There's nothing about it in Henslowe's diary, but all the plays weren't commissioned by Henslowe.

CHUCK. But Chettle was just a hack, and you say that the play is brilliant.

WINSLOW. Now, look: suppose that nothing had survived except the weaker plays of John Webster, that we knew nothing about his great tragedies. Who could possibly imagine their somber magnificence—like a catafalque of rich brocade? Who could imagine from the pinchbeck of the worst of John Ford his alembicated lyric pathos? Should we not have thought of both of these writers as hacks?

CHUCK. There's a good lyric in *The Devil's Law Case:*

"Vain the ambition of kings,
Who seek by trophies and dead things
To leave a living name behind,
And weave but nets to catch the wind."

*He reads poetry well, not at all in the tone of
his conversation.*

WINSLOW. A few good passages, yes—but there
are good things in Chettle, too—and why should not
Chettle, too, have written a masterpiece? We have,
after all, only one play of his that's not a collabora-
tion: a tragedy of revenge, *Hoffman*, and it's not
unlike the one I've discovered—the same imagery,
the same mannerisms of style.

CHUCK. How would you date your play?

WINSLOW. A reference to Queen Elizabeth as still
alive shows that it must be earlier than 1603—and
Chettle must have died at some point between 1603
and 1607. And the play is so much superior to
Chettle's other productions that it may well be the
last thing he wrote and the culminating work of
his life. (*With deliberate smiling slyness, as if he
were lecturing to a class.*) But that's not the whole
story. I *don't* think that Chettle was alone in the
authorship of this play. There are passages that
must come from another hand, and I *don't* think it
could have been anyone so relatively inferior as
Middleton or Dekker or Rowley. (*He pauses, but
Chuck does not encourage him by asking who he
thinks this collaborator might be.*) Now, we know

on positive evidence that Chettle had a hand in *Sir Thomas More*—which was also discovered in man-uscript—and you know who else had a hand. The handwriting shows it conclusively.

CHUCK. You mean Shakespeare.

WINSLOW. You'll tell me what you think when you've seen it. There are certain scenes in the play that, it seems to me, could only have been written by Shakespeare.

CHUCK. Where do you see the resemblance?

WINSLOW. Well, you know Shakespeare's mar-vellous nocturnes: the ghost on the battlements at the beginning of *Hamlet*, Iachimo in Imogen's bed-chamber. There's a hair-raising night scene at the beginning of the play. And then there's a scene with the clown that seems to me unmistakable. It's just the kind of thing that Shakespeare wrote for his favorite comic actor Will Kempe.

CHUCK. Who's your clown?

WINSLOW. Terry Moran.

CHUCK. You're running an awful risk. I hope that he turns up sober.

WINSLOW. Oh, Terry's a glorious clown. I al-ways had him do the comics when we read the plays aloud in class—he had everybody in stitches.

CHUCK. And Spooky Simms is your villain, I understand.

WINSLOW. Not exactly the villain—a spy.

CHUCK. Aren't you carrying type-casting a little too far? How did you get him to play it?

FRAN. He doesn't want to be left out of anything, and he wants to propitiate Father.

The door bell rings, and Fran goes to answer it.

WINSLOW. Oh, Ned's not so bad as that. And he has one superb speech—one of the best in the play. He does have a real love of literature—in spite of what I can't help feeling is a rather pedantic tendency to pick away at texts and attempt to find all kinds of things in them that the author couldn't possibly have put there. That's a fashion that will soon pass. The voice of the great poets will always drown out their analysts!

Fran comes back with Spooky Simms. He is pale and blond, in his late thirties. Correct college-campus garb: white buttoned-down shirt, conservative tie, trousers and jacket of different materials. He has earned his college nickname by a certain slightly creepy quality.

WINSLOW. Hello, Ned. I've just made what I think are some interesting discoveries about our play.—And you, I understand, have been doing some very exciting work on Yeats.

Spooky salutes Chuck and Fran, but Chuck does not respond.

SPOOKY. I've cracked *The Wild Swans at Coole!*

WINSLOW (*smiling*). Not irreparably, I hope.

SPOOKY. I started off on the wrong track: I was looking for symbols of the Mass.

CHUCK. Yeats was a Protestant with a leaning to-

ward Theosophy. He was all against Catholic Ire-
land.

SPOOKY. That was only incidental criticism. I
think there can be no question that he was always
a crypto-Catholic. I could show it to you in poem
after poem: Kiltartan Cross in the *Airman,* the
Nativity in *Among School Children.* But that's not
what's important here—it's the homosexual thing.

CHUCK. What homosexual thing?

SPOOKY. Oh, my dear boy, it's all there! The
poem is crammed with homosexual allusions. The
wild swans—Wilde—remember that Yeats knew
Oscar—we don't know how well. And swans—that
refers to Proust. *Swann's Way* had come out in
1919—just six years before the poem.

CHUCK. Yeats didn't read French.

SPOOKY. He had his ways: Arthur Symons.

WINSLOW. There's the phone. (*It has not been
heard.*) Excuse me, Ned. Rehearsal tomorrow, remember.

SPOOKY. I'll be there.

Winslow goes into the study, closing the door.

CHUCK. That's all a lot of crap, Spooky.

SPOOKY. Well, give it a close reading. Are the
wild swans really swans? There's no mention of
any females—nothing about eggs or cygnets? (*He
reads flatly, with no regard for the poetry.*)

"Unwearied still, lover by lover,
They paddle in the cool
Companionable streams or climb the air."

"Lover by lover," you notice.

"Among what rushes will they build,
By what lake's edge or pool
Delight men's eyes when I awake some day
To find they have flown away?"

"Delight *men's* eyes." You see. The swans are, of course, young men, and Yeats is quite specific about them. He tells us that there are "nine and fifty swans"—that is, fifty-nine young men. This is of great biographical interest. And then, of course, the wild swans of Hans Christian Andersen, who were all, you remember, young princes. And Andersen himself was a homosexual.

CHUCK. I thought Yeats was a confirmed hetero. What about Maud Gonne?

SPOOKY. Maud Gonne was six feet tall and had a square jaw like a New York policeman. Did you ever see a portrait of her? A bull dyke, if ever you saw one.

CHUCK. I won't buy that.

SPOOKY. You haven't seen the whole argument. I'm doing a paper on it for *Contemporary Explications*.

CHUCK. I don't expect to see it.

SPOOKY. Of course, your discipline should really have been Classics. It's a pity they're so weak at Hillsdale. You had to do it all yourself and be practically an autodidact. Do you have any time for them with your teaching load?

CHUCK. Yes: I'm translating Pindar.

SPOOKY. From what point of view?

CHUCK. From the point of view of putting him into English.

SPOOKY. In verse?

CHUCK. Yes, of course.

SPOOKY. Isn't that rather an ambitious project?

CHUCK. It's never been adequately done, and I'm certain that I can do it.

SPOOKY. I admire your self-confidence, Chucky, but even if you can, I'm not sure that such an undertaking, quite outside your own field, which is English, is the best possible qualification for advancement in the academic world.

CHUCK. To hell with the academic world!

SPOOKY. I suppose you must have felt the temptation to become a professional athlete. I understand you've had offers from some of the big teams. You've been doing such splendid work as coach here. It's such a pity you lost the big game.

CHUCK. Oh, go screw yourself, Spooky—that's the only way you'll ever make it.

SPOOKY. In the first place, if you don't mind, Chucky, I'd rather you wouldn't call me by that nickname in public, as you did the other day. It might have a bad effect on the Freshmen—to whom, after all, I'm responsible in a way that you are not.

CHUCK. Don't worry about what you're called. They'll soon—

FRAN. Come, come: this isn't a play by Albee!

SPOOKY. I'm afraid I must go, Fran. But what I really called about was to ask you to go to the John Cage concert.

FRAN. A fun evening! Funny noises or no noise at all.

SPOOKY. One can't be sure that there isn't something in it. One ought to give it a hearing.

FRAN. OK.

SPOOKY. Dinner first: I'll come to get you at seven.

FRAN. Make it twenty minutes past. I'll have to rehearse the Ophelia scene with Father.

SPOOKY. Very good. Seven twenty, Saturday.— Good-bye, Chucky.

Chuck does not acknowledge this. Fran leaves the room with Spooky, accompanying him to the front door. Chuck looks after him with angry disgust. He picks up Mad *magazine, glances at it, then throws it down. In the meantime, while Spooky Simms is putting on his coat, we hear this conversation from the hall.*

SPOOKY. I thought I handled that with dignity.

FRAN. He *is* very difficult. But you have to make allowances.

SPOOKY. Yes, of course.—Well, till Saturday.

He goes out, and Fran returns.

CHUCK. He's getting ready to put the skids under me and your father both.

During the conversation that follows, he walks

*up and down the room. Fran goes back to her
chair.*

FRAN. I'm going to work on him Saturday.

CHUCK. Butter him up under false pretenses!

FRAN. That's academic life.

CHUCK. I insulted him just now.

FRAN. And *I* have to try to defend you.

CHUCK. They'd fire me anyway.

FRAN. I'm trying to save you.

CHUCK. I'm on a higher level than they are, so
they hate me.

FRAN. Well, why don't you at least look decent?

CHUCK. What's the use?

FRAN. Well, for one thing, I'd enjoy seeing you
more.

CHUCK. You don't give a damn about me anyway.

FRAN. I wouldn't worry about you if I didn't.

CHUCK. I tried cleaning up on your account, and
I never got anywhere with you. What's the use?

FRAN. That lasted about ten days.

CHUCK. I thought you promised me something.

FRAN. Conditions weren't favorable then.

CHUCK. You'd always find conditions unfavor-
able.

FRAN. Then you get sulky and disagreeable.

CHUCK. I still am.

FRAN. Well, don't take it out on other people.
Why should you be so rude to everybody?

CHUCK. You're pretty sassy yourself.

FRAN. I'm part of the picture here. You're just barely hanging on.

CHUCK. And your delightful but dotty old father. Trying to make him do Freshmen English—wasting time with those delinquents that can't read or write till they decide to drop out at the end of the first term. That's where they've got *me*.

FRAN. I don't see why you didn't go in for Greek.

CHUCK. No demand for it, and I'm an even more irritant burr for the kind of people that teach it. And by taking on a frankly menial job, I'm free to devote my time to it.

FRAN. I don't think they can make Father teach freshmen.

CHUCK. They'll do everything possible to crab his act. Spooky's building up a department of anti-humanistic little operators like himself—handpicked as inferior to him. And you can't go lower than that. He doesn't want a brilliant entertainer showing the students that literature can be made exciting. He doesn't even care about the prestige of the college. Your father used to be known as the genius who sold Shakespeare to the football men. Now Spooky has flunked half the team for not following his Talmudic interpretations. That's why we lost the Middlebury game. God help Winky Carter this year if he won't believe that Yeats was a pansy. He's our prize player but a pretty smart guy.

Fran. I'm going to make that point. I think I can save Father's lectures.

Chuck. What will be the price? Your hand in marriage?

Fran. You let me worry about that.

Chuck. I never can have a wife because I'll never have permanent tenure.

Fran. You've done everything possible to prevent it.

Chuck. I'm living like a goddam monk working over a classical manuscript, and I can't get anywhere with *you.*

Fran. I've taught you to blow your nose.

Chuck. Do you think that Spooky's a pansy himself?

Fran (*shrugs*). He's a professional mama's boy.

Chuck. With a tiny little power drive.—Mrs. Simms is in the play too?

Fran. She's Queen Constance of Aragon.

Chuck. God! I'm afraid it's going to be a howl. —Whenever I see Mrs. Simms, I'm glad that I don't have a mother. But you had a nice one, didn't you?

Fran. Yes.

Chuck (*stopping in front of the portrait*). That's her, is it?

Fran. Yes—when she'd just come out.

Chuck. She was a pupil of your father's?

Fran. She never really went to college—but she audited a course of his at Barnard. It was quite a romantic affair. Her family were all against her

marrying him. He was just a poor English instructor. But they were crazy about one another.

CHUCK. They say she died of living at Hillsdale.
I've never understood why *you* stayed here. In my
case, it was the best I could do. They gave me a
scholarship.

FRAN. You got your M.A. at Harvard.

CHUCK. And they hated me there worse than
here.—But you could have gone to Bryn Mawr or
anywhere.

FRAN. I had to stick by Father. He's never really
gotten over Mother's death. I thought that he was
going to die of despair. He sometimes still thinks
she's around. They spent their honeymoon on a
walking trip in England. That's why he went there
last summer. He found some valuable books when
he took that hike with my mother, and he sometimes talks as if she'd been with him when he discovered this manuscript. She was always sure that
some day he'd do something outstandingly brilliant.

CHUCK. And I was a bastard and an orphan!

FRAN. You mustn't tell people that too often.

CHUCK. That's a very poor joke.

FRAN. What joke?

CHUCK. Orphan-often.

FRAN. That wasn't a joke—it was accidental.
Don't have such a chip on your shoulder.

CHUCK. Why not?—What I meant was I can't
even imagine growing up in a loving family. And
don't you show off, yourself, with that coming-out

stuff either. Your people had it made. I had to do everything myself.

FRAN. Don't give me all that again.

Winslow comes in from the study.

WINSLOW. A terrible blow has fallen! Winky Carter has flunked Physics a second time, and his work is below standard. Ned Simms won't even give him a B minus.

CHUCK (*to Fran*). What was I just telling you?

WINSLOW. Now they won't let him take part in any extra-curricular activities. It wasn't even worth arguing with the Dean.

CHUCK. They're sabotaging the play. This isn't the first evidence of it.

WINSLOW. Oh, no: I don't think so. But what are we going to do? We've got to get someone for Giovanni, and the opening's only five days off!

CHUCK. Sam Defoe?

FRAN. Oh, no: he's a stick, and he mumbles. When he played Hippolytus in *Phaedra*, nobody could possibly imagine why Phaedra was so crazy about him.

WINSLOW. You made quite a terrifying Bosola in *The Duchess of Malfi*, Chuck, and this part needs a certain brutality.

CHUCK. Get it up in five days?

FRAN. You know Pindar and Homer by heart. I don't see why you couldn't do it.

WINSLOW. Yes, Chuck: you're just the man. I was never really satisfied with Winky, and I'm sure that you can give it the noble fire and the angry strength held in reserve that is what the part demands.

CHUCK. Well, the Middlebury game is over. Let me read the script.

Winslow dashes out into the study.

CHUCK. What do I do in the play?

FRAN. You try to carry out a hideous revenge. You're out to kill the man who murdered your father, but you get killed yourself instead.

CHUCK. That would be just my luck.—Who are you?

FRAN. I'm your girlfriend—so take a bath before rehearsals.

CHUCK. What happens to you?

FRAN. I go crazy on account of you're killed.

CHUCK. A likely story!

Winslow comes back with the script.

WINSLOW. Can you read it right away? There's not a moment to lose! But please don't talk about it. All the actors have been pledged to secrecy.

CHUCK. I'll let you know tonight.

He takes the script and goes out, without further ceremony.

WINSLOW. I believe that Chuck could be splendid!

FRAN. Do you think he can act with Spooky?

WINSLOW. Oh, both of them are dedicated souls. Their approaches, of course, are different; but where it's a question of poetry, such differences are unimportant. I know that Ned doesn't approve

of *my* methods, but he's glad to appear in my play
—in the play. The competition between theories of
interpretation belongs to the small academic world
—a matter of parochial jealousies. On the great stage
of Elizabethan drama, all such rivalries must be forgotten!

FRAN. I hope you're right.—I must get on that
damn sociology.

WINSLOW. How abominably they write!

FRAN. You said it.

*She goes out by the door into the hall. Winslow
turns to the portrait.*

WINSLOW. If only Daphne were here! I feel that
she *will* be with me on our opening night!

"Oh, lyric love, half-angel and half bird
And all a wonder and a wild desire"—

*He puts his hands over his eyes and begins to
sob.*

"Cover her face; mine eyes dazzle; she died"—

*The telephone in the study is heard. He turns
briskly and goes back into the study.*

THE NIGHT OF THE PLAY

In front of the curtain, Professor Edgar J. Creech and his assistant Warren Tisdale. They are wearing their hats and overcoats, and both carry umbrellas.

Tisdale (*soft-spoken, tactful and very deferential toward Creech*). I hope that that plane didn't —shake you up.

Creech (*loud, harsh, nasal Middle-Western voice*). I never let anything shake me up. I've been through much worse than that. I went by freighter to Uppsala in the middle of December once. I had to examine the only existing quarto of *The Merry Wench of Westminster*. The only time I could get away: Christmas holidays. I had to go by way of the Baltic—too expensive by train. Roughest voyage I ever had.

Tisdale. What a marvelous edition you made of the *Wench*. I wonder whether this trip will be equally rewarding.

Creech. I doubt it.

Tisdale. You're evidently the only expert who's taken the trouble to come here. But then, of course, at the present time, you're the only real expert in the field.—One wonders why Winslow hasn't shown it to anyone.

CREECH. One may well wonder.

TISDALE. He now thinks that Chettle wrote it. If it's as poor stuff as what we have of Chettle, it was hardly worth the finding.

CREECH. All texts are of equal value—*if* they're authentic.

TISDALE. If they're authentic, of course.—I wonder whether he knows you're here.

CREECH. He will when he sees me.

TISDALE. You know him?

CREECH. I heard him lecture once.

TISDALE. What impression did you get of him?

CREECH. A mountebank.

TISDALE. Most popular lecturers are mountebanks. Scholars like yourself are almost extinct—they will be when *you* are gone. Who is there to take your place?

CREECH. Nobody.

TISDALE. I've at least mastered your method—I hope. (*A suggestive pause, but no answer.*) Though I haven't your encyclopaedic learning. But someone will have to be found to carry on your tradition in the George Hamilton Pratt chair.

CREECH. *You* couldn't carry it on, if that's what you're thinking of. Not only don't you have the knowledge, you don't have the necessary character. Scholarship needs lifelong persistence and uninterrupted application. I've refused to give courses for thirty-five years—nowdays I hardly even see graduate students. But you've become a popular teacher yourself. I don't say you're a mountebank yet, but you probably will be eventually. I'm not leaving you my blessing for the chair, if that's what you're hinting at.

TISDALE (*shocked and crushed*). May I ask who will have that distinction?

CREECH. Nobody: the chair will be abolished.

TISDALE. How *can* it be abolished?

CREECH. I've told Pratt I want it abolished, and the money to go thereafter to adding to the Elizabethan collection and keeping my editions in print.

TISDALE. Isn't that something for the college to decide?

CREECH. Pratt's on the Board of Trustees and the principal contributor of funds. If it hadn't been for him, the little place would have folded long ago. They've got to do what he tells them.—Have you got the tickets?

Tisdale mutely produces them. They take off their hats and coats. A student usher from Hillsdale comes out on the stage right, tears off the stubs and takes the professors to two seats at the extreme right of the stage. During the scene backstage that follows, which they are not supposed to see, Creech examines the program and looks around at the theater, without speaking and in cold indifference. Tisdale, disappointed and miffed, constrainedly studies the program. When the performance proper begins, Creech is seen assiduously taking notes.

SCENE III

Backstage. Winslow, in the medieval costume of the Duke, is nervously inspecting the stage and the properties. Fran, in the costume of the Duke's niece Violante, comes to him from a door on the right.

FRAN. Did you know that Edgar J. Creech is here?

WINSLOW. Who?

FRAN. That Elizabethan expert from the West Coast—Edgar J. Creech.

WINSLOW (*startled and rather upset*). Edgar Creech from California?

FRAN. He's flown on to see the play. Ned Simms just told me.

WINSLOW. Oh, I wish I could see him first! I'd like to have a little talk with him.

FRAN. It's too late for that now.

WINSLOW. Yes. Dear me! I hope he doesn't expect too much—in the way of textual scrutiny.

FRAN. He doesn't look as if he did. I've peeked at him through the curtain.

WINSLOW. He's a very rigorous scholar, and there are passages I'm still not sure of.—I've always thought him a little uninspired.

FRAN. Don't let him throw you off. You can always make anything go. The students are all for you.

WINSLOW. Is Terry Moran on hand?

FRAN. Yes.

WINSLOW. What sort of condition is he in?

FRAN. He'll be tight as a tick, I'm afraid, unless something is done about him. You'd better have a talk with him now.

Terry Moran appears. He is dressed as the Clown and quite high.

TERRY (*clapping Winslow on the shoulder*). What ho, my good lord! I come from Joe Turucci's Mermaid Bar, where a goodly company of whoreson knaves do break jests and quaff canary. They drink to my lord's noble health. Marry come up with a wannion!

WINSLOW. All right, Terry. Are you sure of your lines? Let's not have any improvements tonight. The play's bawdy enough already. Remember Hamlet's admonition: "And let those who play your clowns speak no more than is set down for them."

TERRY. Have no fear, my good lord.
This jackanapes will not bebawd the stage,
Although the greatest clown of this or any other goddam age!
(*Producing a pint of whisky*) Wilt drink with me, good Duke?

Fran quietly takes the bottle away from him.

WINSLOW. Try to sober up, Terry—or I'll have

to cut that scene we have together. And I know you can be so good in it. You don't want to spoil the performance. Please.

TERRY (*in his natural voice*). Don't worry, sir, I'll be all right.

WINSLOW. Go out and get a breath of air. These tiny little dressing rooms are stifling.

Spooky and Chuck appear in the costumes of Perfidio and Giovanni di Procida.

TERRY (*gesturing towards Spooky*).

There struts the horrid villain, mean and base!

Dids't ever dig so sickening a face?

WINSLOW. This is not a melodrama, Terry, but a tragedy of revenge. You've never seen the whole of the play. (*To Fran*) Take him out into the open air.

She leads Terry out.

WINSLOW (*to Chuck*). Are the Skeletons all sober?

CHUCK. More or less.

During the conversation that follows, seven Skeletons straggle in. They wear black dominoes, with the bones in white. They are carrying their skull-masks that fit over their heads. One has a large ewer, and two carry musical instruments.

SPOOKY (*pretending to joke with the Skeletons*). Well, boys, if you'd tried that costume on Middlebury, you might have scared them and not lost the game.

The Skeletons give him only sour looks.

WINSLOW (*after looking the Skeletons over, to Chuck*). Do the curtains for the inner stage work?

CHUCK. I don't think we've tried them out to-night.

WINSLOW. They got stuck at the last rehearsal. We'd better see about them.

He goes behind the stage. Spooky addresses Chuck in a quiet but distinct voice, loud enough for the Skeletons to hear. They soon begin to listen attentively.

SPOOKY. Well, old boy, you've got some good news coming to you! (*Chuck looks at him suspiciously and apprehensively.*) You might as well hear it right away. You've been called, as the preachers say, to Steep Rock College in Tennessee. I had an interview with the President a month ago. They wanted someone for their English Department—their best man got killed skiing—and I recommended you. I've had a feeling that you were hoping to do Classics here—

CHUCK. No, I wasn't.

SPOOKY. Well, there's less and less call for them nowadays, and old Thaddeus Winterfield takes care of the few students that want them. Even when he retires, you could hardly take his place, because, unfortunately, you haven't the academic qualifications. You know the situation here. There really isn't any place for you. You're frankly hostile to the policies of our department, and we've made the decision, with much regret, that we'll have to let you go. On the Rock, as they call it, you'll be supreme. You can formulate your own policies. To be sure, it's a bit isolated—a touch of Mount Athos, they say. But it's perfectly accessible by ski-lift, and there's a certain dedicated spirit—teaching those mountaineers. I think it will appeal to your idealism. And then, they need an athletic coach. The President is very ambitious for the athletic side of the college. He says that the students, in general, are splendid physical specimens. The defeat of your team this fall was regrettable, but at the Rock you'll have fresh material. You can teach them football from the ground up—you won't be threatened by serious competition. And the salary is not contemptible. They're handsomely endowed, you know. You couldn't have a better stepping-stone to what I hope will be higher things.

CHUCK. Going up in the ski-lift, you mean?

SPOOKY (*self-consciously laughing*). Oh, in that sense, I think Steep Rock is high enough.

The first bell to give the actors notice rings. Chuck says nothing further and walks out. The Skeletons go out on the left to take their places on the inner stage.

A SKELETON. Did you hear that? He's firing Chuck.

SECOND SKELETON. It was all Spooky's own damn fault that we had such a lousy season. He disqualified half the team last spring.

Mrs. Simms, Spooky's mother, appears from

*the dressing room. She is dressed as Queen Con-
stance of Aragon and wears a Spanish mantilla.
She is a sharp New England woman, who wears
an old-fashioned pince-nez and speaks with extreme precision.*

SPOOKY. I've just broken the news to Chuck
Chambers.

MRS. SIMMS. How did he take it?

SPOOKY. Not very well, I'm afraid. He has a certain resentment against me. I hope it won't upset
him in his part.

MRS. SIMMS. It'll be a good riddance so far as
I'm concerned. That young man gives me more
trouble than anybody else at the library. He keeps
the books out for weeks and pays no attention
to my notices. When he brings them back, they're
all scribbled up. He's also exceedingly insolent.

SPOOKY. I know he is, Mother, but you have to
remember his unfortunate circumstances—his birth
and his early struggles. And you mustn't forget that,
in the play itself, you and he are supposed to be
on the same side.

The bell rings again.

SCENE IV

In front of the curtain. Winslow, in the costume of the Duke, with his usual horn-rimmed glasses, which now give him something of the look of Greco's portrait of the bearded and bespectacled Cardinal de Guevara. He reads, with vivacity and gusto, a prologue spoken in his own character.

WINSLOW.
In cold October, yet with blood aglow,
Like Borrow's footloose vagrant Lavengro,
Undaunted by damp mists and murky mires,
I trudged through lank old England's northern shires
By ways no blaring billboards yet had marred,
By gentle lanes no motor-horns had jarred,
Waked only by the hunter's ringing halloo;
The grass still green when ours is sere and sallow;
Old houses that must harbor each its ghost;
Old cosy country inns in which mine host
Serves mellow ale and steak-and-kidney pie,
A faithful fire of coals bright burning nigh.

So faring, with a rucksack on my back,
Beyond the ignorant tourist's beaten track,

I chanced upon a lovely town at last
That seemed a remnant from the vanished past:
No Boots, no modern bars, no petrol smell;
A faceless castle little but a shell;
A church with belfry steeple-lopped and squared,
The ravages of Cromwell scarce repaired—
Blackened without and mortal chill within;
The sacristan lugubrious and lean;
Old tombs of nobles lying blurred and chipped,
Squat Norman arches crouching in the crypt.

'Twas here that, after supping hungrily,
On buttered scones, sardines on toast, and tea,
Served by firm-bosomed lasses, never slimmed,
Sloe-eyed and pert-nosed such as Hogarth limned,
I found a bookshop piled with ancient trash
Dragged from dark attics for a bit of cash;
The wheezing dealer, bleary-eyed and sad,
Dull-witted, hardly knowing what he had.
Yet, grubbing there in dust, I brought to light
These precious items, buried out of sight:
Clarissa, London, seventeen fifty-one,
"Printed for"—that is, by—"S. Richardson";
A handful of Marprelate tracts that span
The comic quarrel of priest with Puritan.
And now the dealer—dimly perchance noting
My eyes agleam, my exclamations gloating—
A manuscript part-crumbled did produce:
Elizabethan loops and curlicues
Of which he could make nothing, but to me

The True and Lamentable Tragedie
Of sad Palermo's Duke, a work unknown,
No date, no author—left for me alone!
Curbing excitement—what a day of killings!—
I bought the lot for two pounds and eight shillings;
And all night pored with ever-growing glee,
Since years before I'd won my Ph.D.
On Henry Chettle—not an obscure hack,
As some suppose who true discernment lack,
But one who brought a touch of somber glory
To German *Hoffman's* harsh and bloody story.
I recognized his favorite darkling phrases:
The purple blood, the windy blasts—where blazes
A fury of Satanic eloquence—
In *Hoffman*, still half-smouldering, though intense,
Which, in *Palermo*, might perchance arouse
A mounting horror that would rock the house!

This we present tonight, as best we may:
Our faults, our fallings-short forgive, we pray.
I have said that Chettle must have penned this
    piece,
And yet *two* pens at work one plainly sees.
Was Chettle all unaided, we demand,
Or had he, then, the help of some far greater hand?

The subject of *The Duke of Palermo* I have
found to be more or less historical: the rising of
Sicily against the French—the so-called Sicilian
Vespers—at the end of the thirteenth century. For

the purposes of this performance, we are forced
to omit the subplot, which, brilliant though it is
in its way, has, nevertheless—as is often the case
in the Elizabethan dramas—little relevance to the
main story and which would involve us in too long
an evening.

He bows and withdraws.

SCENE V

A trumpet call. The girl who plays Lucia, a small brunette, passes across the stage with a placard reading: "A Castle in Italy." Half-way across, she stops and displays it, then walks out at the other side.

The curtain goes up. Chuck and Terry, as Prince Giovanni di Procida and the Clown, at the front of a darkened stage. Terry-Clown holds up a lantern, and Chuck-Giovanni looks about him as if at a high spacious chamber.

CHUCK-GIOVANNI.
Here where my father, German Conradin,
Kept kingly state and ruled with equal hand
Jerusalem and sun-bak'd Sicily;
Where once in childhood, munching sugarplums,
I frisk'd upon the flower'd terraces,
Chas'd butterflies and lov'd to play crusader
With mimic weapons, heedless of the wars
That France and Italy in hate did wage
'Gainst one another. After twenty years
I come again, Giovanni of Procida,
A poor and petty prince, to find all dark,
Decayed and cobwebb'd, smelling dank of death,
Ruin'd and robb'd by Charles the Angevin,
Vile Frank, the slayer of my noble sire.

A thunderclap.
Methinks Jove rages at th' abhorrent deed!
Hark how he thunders!

A prolonged flash of lighting illuminates the scene, revealing, on the inner stage, a banquet table, at which five of the Skeletons are sitting, two on either side, and at the head, facing the audience, the host, who lacks a skull. This skull, which wears a crown—also facing the audience —is set before the Skeleton to which it belongs. All are grasping large goblets, which rest on the table. Behind and to the right of the headless host, stands the cupbearer with his ewer. The two musicians stand, to the fore, on either side of the inner stage.

CHUCK-GIOVANNI.

Look there! What do I see?

TERRY-CLOWN. A deadman's banquet, by'r lady!
Let's hence 'fore they ask us to drink with them!

CHUCK-GIOVANNI.

Draw nigh and light this grisly spectacle.

Terry-Clown holds up the lantern but does not approach too near.

CHUCK-GIOVANNI.

What hollow sconces and dull orbs are these
That, mouldering, sit mumchance in this place?
What vacant cheer and dismal revelry?
Sure Charles of Anjou rigged this ghostly show,
Made thus our banquet hall a charnel-house,
In mockery of my father's majesty.

There sit the guests, there stands the cupbearer,
There the musicians with their tuneless strings,
As many an evening, creeping from my bed
And peeping from the arras, I have seen
A richly clad and courtly company,
Wittily jesting as the wine went round,
My father leading all in gay discourse.

TERRY-CLOWN. I' faith, were those fleshless chaps
to drain a cup, 'twould splash bare ribs and never
bring a belk!

Thunder and lightning.

CHUCK-GIOVANNI.
But look: that skull doth bear a rusted crown!
Draw nigher.

Terry-Clown reluctantly does so.

               'Tis the crown my father wore!
His lordly head, lopped by the Angevin—
Faith's temple, wisdom's tower. But he bore it
Too high for such a crouching beast to brook.

Thunder somewhat fainter.

THE CROWNED SKULL.
My son, first scion of my loins.

CHUCK-GIOVANNI.

                      It speaks.

TERRY-CLOWN. If I must be with bones, godsookers, I would rather they kept silence!

CHUCK-GIOVANNI.
Be still. (*To the Skull*) Speak on.

THE SKULL.   My son, thou
    knowest well

How, worsted by French Charles at Tagliacozzo,
For that our gluttonous troops had turned to
    plunder,
Leaving me ill-defended, I was ta'en,
Condemned as a base traitor and beheaded.
But now this head, dissever'd from its frame,
Set here for scorn, doth still defy its foe
And bids its seed take vengeance. Let no even
Her curtains draw on our fair Sicily
That brings you not the nearer to just vengeance
Against her ravisher and my murderer.
Long have I waited thee. The hour is come
Foretold me ere my death by birds of omen,
Black messengers, in croakèd syllables
To swear my squander'd blood should leap again.
Behold it burns in thee. I cannot kiss thee
With these foul chops, but proudly hail thy coming.
Now swift away! Seek out Palermo's Duke,
Who Charles's insolence would fain rebuke—
Stanch friend, who mid these ills which others whelm
Our honor guards in Charles's bloodied realm.
Avenge, avenge, avenge!
      The Skeletons (*raising their goblets, as if to
    drink to Giovanni's success*).
                         Avenge, avenge!
    Chuck-Giovanni (*falling on his knees*).
Father, I fly to seek the Duke's support.
A sennight sees me at Palermo's court!
    He picks up the Crowned Skull.
And thou poor head, be ever by my side

To look upon those deeds no Frenchman dare
   deride.

   Thunder. The stage goes dark.

   *Spotlight on Tisdale and Creech. Tisdale, now
   angry with Creech, is prepared to take an opposite line from him.*

TISDALE. Conradin had no issue. He was the last
of the Hohenstaufens. Giovanni di Procida was not
his son. But of course the Elizabethans were care-
less about such matters.

CREECH. What's more serious is that the expression
"godsookers" isn't found as early as Chettle. It first
occurs in Buckingham's *Rehearsal:* 1672.

TISDALE. Buckingham can't have invented it,
though. It's the same thing as "gadzooks," which
is all through the Elizabethans.

CREECH. It is *not* the same thing. And why that
Alexandrine at the end?

TISDALE. They did write them as early as that.

CREECH. Not like that at the end of a scene.

TISDALE. Mightn't the Spenserian stanza perhaps
set a precedent for doing so?

No reply from Creech.

SCENE VI

Lucia crosses the stage with a placard which reads: "Palermo. Palace of the Duke."
The Duke is seen at his writing table.

WINSLOW-DUKE.
In what cribb'd crush'd condition do I dwell
Beneath these coffer'd roofs which hous'd my sires,
Behind gates, pillar'd with our plumèd arms,
That now we scarce dare pass lest some foul insult
From jeering Frank deride our ducal state.
They flout us and degrade us. We are slaves.
We slink like timid mice that fear grimalkin
Who preened as fierce as falcons in our pride.
Our nobles must run errands for low strangers;
The flower of our youth, clapp'd in dark pantries,
Must turn the spit like scullions, fetch rare cates
For gibbering fribbles, while they sup themselves
On scraps and orts. They must e'en comb the fens
For creaking frogs, the fields for slimèd snails
That furnish the pale Franks their filthy fare.
They rob the poor and pill the rich, ransack
All Sicily for the coin to pay their riots
And sate their lusts. They search the very huts
Of those sweet shepherds of Theocritus
Who pipe to their placid flocks beside the sea.

39

—Ah, would Enceladus, the swarthy Titan
Who sleeps in Etna's bowels might belk forth
His burning hail and bury with these tyrants
All that was once most great in Sicily
And now is brought to measliness! Or might
Some young and molten-marrowed champion,
Whose fiery words could blister men like lava,
Burst forth and blast our people to rebellion!
I am too old to fulminate this foray.
    A Servant enters.
    SERVANT.
A friar would have speech with you, my lord.
    WINSLOW-DUKE.
Whence comes he?
    SERVANT.
                From Messina, my good lord.
    WINSLOW-DUKE.
A friend or foe? What thinkest thou?
    SERVANT.
                       I know not.
His dark eyes burn like coals, his breath comes
   short,
As if he were a-fever'd.
    WINSLOW-DUKE.
                   Search him well.
Perchance he flees Messina, where the French
Do now most mightily prevail. If so,
I must protect him. But make sure he be not
Some fell assassin in a friar's garb.
    SERVANT.
He bears beneath his robe some bulky object.

WINSLOW-DUKE.
A weapon? Look to this.
                                        I will, my lord.
  He leaves by a door on the right. Fran-Violante
  enters at the Duke's left through the curtains that
  mask the inner stage.
  FRAN-VIOLANTE.
A letter from Lucia, good mine uncle,
By night and slyness smuggled out of Naples
By our shrewd Sicilian fisher. Much I fear
Lest she herself be spied on, apprehended,
And ne'er fly back to us, our pretty bird
That pipes so linnet-sweet yet hops as wary
As any sparrow foraging for crumbs.
  WINSLOW-DUKE.
He is too confident, the Angevin,
Too dull to see what stirs, too deaf to hear
The mutterings that do mount beneath his throne,
Like some dim pharos loading a tall cliff
Which the sea, storming, loudly undermines.
—What news from Naples?
  FRAN-VIOLANTE.
                              Charles prepares his ships
To ascend the Rhone, snatch Arles, then launch
  a fleet
Against Byzance, and make himself brute master
Of all the Mediterranean—
  The Servant reappears.
  SERVANT.
The friar, my lord—he bears an ebon box,
And in that box a hollow skull—no weapons.

WINSLOW-DUKE.

Such grim reminders the Franciscans cherish.
Admit him.

The Servant ushers in Chuck-Giovanni, disguised as a Franciscan monk. He carries a large black box.

CHUCK-GIOVANNI.

Hail, good duke.

WINSLOW-DUKE.

What wouldst thou
with me?

CHUCK-GIOVANNI.

My lord, I do but crave a privy word,
Not to be witnessèd nor overheard.

WINSLOW-DUKE.

This is my lady niece. You may speak as free
When she is by as you may speak with me.

CHUCK-GIOVANNI.

Then hark, my lord. No holy friar I!
(*He throws off his hood.*)
Not one who begs in dim humility,
Not one who drips Christ's pity, but a prince
Who, clad in russet, comes to claim revenge
And princely cloth of gold. Look here, my lord!

He opens the ebony box and produces the Crowned Skull. Fran-Violante registers astonishment and horror; Winslow-Duke eyes it more coolly.

WINSLOW-DUKE.

Why, what is this?

CHUCK-GIOVANNI.
                    The head of Conradin—
And I his son, Giovanni of Procida!
    WINSLOW-DUKE (*grasping his hands*).
I knew thee as a babe! How cam'st thou here?
    CHUCK-GIOVANNI.
I come with Spanish Pedro at my back,
Who claims usurpèd Sicily by the right
Of Constance, Manfred's daughter, his fierce queen.
She sails in secret and should meet me here.
    The Servant enters.
    SERVANT.
A lady waits without.
    CHUCK-GIOVANNI.
                    Hath she green eyes,
A queenly carriage and an emerald ring?
    SERVANT.
All three she hath, good father.
    WINSLOW-DUKE.
                    Let her come in.
    Mrs. Simms-Constance makes a stiff entrance,
as the Servant turns to escort her.
    WINSLOW-DUKE.
Hail, madam, gracious queen.
    MRS. SIMMS-CONSTANCE.
                    All hail, good Duke.
I come to claim mine own, to wrest my realm,
Rough Sicily, from the Angevin.
    (*Seeing the skull*)
                    Why, what's this?

CHUCK-GIOVANNI.
The festering presence of my murder'd sire,
Who calls to vengeance.
    MRS. SIMMS-CONSTANCE.
                          Ah, 'tis well, 'tis well.
Me Manfred also calls, Tarentum's Prince,
Conradin's Regent, lord of Sicily,
And rightful Emperor of Italy.
In sleep he did me visit, bade me haste,
With strong and tearing talons, eagle-like,
To gripe and gut these Franks as they do frogs!
    WINSLOW-DUKE.
An eagle? Nay, a crested cockatrice,
As once I saw it on an arid plain
Transfix by its horrid look a hunter there,
Who had glimps'd it not before he met its stare.
Had he seen it first, 'twould have been the other
    way:
The man might still be living to this day.
    (*To the audience, falling into his classroom
    habits.*)
If the cockatrice saw you first, you were gone.
    FRAN-VIOLANTE (*whose admiration for Giovanni
has been obvious*).
Will you not partake of some refreshment, Prince—
A venison pasty with some candied quince?
Your dusty journey must have made you dry.
Our cool Sicilian wine—
    CHUCK-GIOVANNI.
                   Nay, do not ply

My tensèd purpose with the dazing draught!
No wavering hand must launch the lethal shaft.
To business now!
    WINSLOW-DUKE.
              Yes, we must lay our schemes.
He nothing braves who only bides and dreams.

    CREECH. "Bulky object." The adjective *bulky*
didn't come into use till the late 1680's.
    TISDALE. I wonder whether "creaking frogs"
may not be a misreading for "croaking frogs."
    CREECH. One would have to see the manuscript.
    TISDALE. If it *is* a misreading—which seems pos-
sible—the manuscript may be authentic.
    *He glances sidelong at Creech, who does not
reply.*

SCENE VII

Placard: "The Duke's Garden." Spooky-Per-
fidio and Fran-Violante. A bench.

FRAN-VIOLANTE.
You do me too much honor, gentle sir,
To come so often to our stricken house,
Where rings no mirth nor music as of old,
Where sunlight scarcely enters.
SPOOKY-PERFIDIO.
                              My sweet lady,
No place is cheerless where your eyes do shine;
There needs no other music where your voice
Sounds softer and more melting than the lute.
FRAN-VIOLANTE.
Your compliments take all too far a flight:
They overshoot the mark.
SPOOKY-PERFIDIO.
                              They fall far short.
Let us sit upon this bench and drink the moonlight.
Bright Luna, how she silvers every leaf!
The trees are hung with tinsel; every stem
And petal is with tinfoil over-ic'd.
Rose, olive, e'en the tremulous mimosa
Scarce stir in this calm air that nothing sways,
Yet waft abroad their aromatic fragrance.

46

In this sad moment, we may envy England
For that upon her thriving state and mart
Another Dian sheds her steady radiance
And warrants peace while Sicily knows it not.
    FRAN-VIOLANTE.
E'en Rome's mad tyrants spake their subjects' tongue.
    Chuck-Giovanni appears and stands listening.
    SPOOKY-PERFIDIO.
And yet I almost think we are irked too much
By these discordant sounds. Were't not the wiser
    course
To learn their Frankish speech, so like to ours,
And thus with courteous grace and argument
Persuade and cozen these unwise invaders,
Who scorn to learn a language not their own.
    CHUCK-GIOVANNI (*coming forward*).
Such were the mark of vile subservience!
Our foes would scorn us for't, believe us bested.
    SPOOKY-PERFIDIO.
Methinks your rebel spirit, my good monk,
Doth ill befit a meek Franciscan's breast.
    CHUCK-GIOVANNI.
Christ drove the money-changers from the temple.
    SPOOKY-PERFIDIO.
Saint Francis tam'd the wolf by loving kindness.
—And now farewell, sweet lady. I must leave you.
If there be aught of service I can render,
Remember that I've won some little credit
With those who harry us, and speak their jargon.
—Good night, good friar.

CHUCK-GIOVANNI (*rather unconvincingly*).
                          A blessing on thee, sir.
   (*When Perfidio has left, to Violante*)
The moon is clear, yet lights it not our darkness
That lurks in arras'd hall and humble cottage.
See how the tall agave whets her spines,
Fierce as that craz'd Bacchante of old Greece
Whose name she bears—who, all unwitting, tore
Her hapless son to tatters and nail'd up
His bleeding head in Dionysus' temple.
So, whetted well and witting well, our blades
Shall hack and rive the mazzard of no kinsman,
His kingly purple stain with purple gore!
   The Duke enters.
   FRAN-VIOLANTE.
I am unquiet, uncle and Giovanni.
I fear Perfidio: he comes too oft
And creeps too close, as if to catch our secrets,
And he doth question me while softly sighing
And pleading with his eyes, as he did woo me.
Anon his glance grows cold, his accents biting,
As when a sudden chill and nipping wind
The canker'd fruit of mellow autumn cuts.
I shrink and tremble then. I loathe his guts.
   WINSLOW-DUKE (*correcting this departure from the text*).—"as at the sting". . .
   FRAN-VIOLANTE.
I shrink and tremble then, as at the sting
Of some much-fawning yet envenom'd thing.

WINSLOW-DUKE.

I find him faithful, though he woos the Franks
As well as thee, so let us have no pranks
That might rebuff him. Bear with him awhile.
It costs but little gratefully to smile,
Avoid offense and never to reveal
We feign a friendship that we do not feel.
Alas, we all must learn now to dissemble,
No matter how we shrink nor how we tremble.
  He withdraws.

CHUCK-GIOVANNI.

The time for trembling's past. Thy father dotes.
Thou hast the hardier spirit, Violante.
Once we are masters here, I mean to wed thee,
And make thee mistress of thy Sicily.

FRAN-VIOLANTE.

And Constance? Wilt thou wrest it from her talons?

CHUCK-GIOVANNI.

The hawk shall have her nest. But I shall stand
Her guard and guarantor, with thee beside me.
These Spaniards flash and brag but we of Italy
By intellect do snuff their filmy flame.
—Violante, with another flame thou burnest.
Thou shalt stand my consort and my counsellor.

FRAN-VIOLANTE.

I have waited long. When I was but a girl,
Medreamt a jet-black stallion pawed the turf
Beside my door and bade me mount and ride him.

CHUCK-GIOVANNI.

'Tis *I* shall ride *thee*.

FRAN-VIOLANTE.

Shall we race abreast,
And see which steed shall give the other best?
CHUCK-GIOVANNI.
That way lies danger. When two horses race,
They strain and jostle for the stopping-place.
Nay, though I spake of reigning side by side,
The mare must carry and the master ride.

TISDALE. The reference to Queen Elizabeth is
quite out of place in the thirteenth century—but of
course the Elizabethans did do those things.

CREECH. The agave is a *Mexican* plant.

TISDALE. Yes, but there are several species, and
some were brought to Europe in the middle of the
sixteenth century. I'm an enthusiastic gardener,
you know, and consequently a bit of a botanist.
They do have agave in Sicily.—What do you make
of the reference to Euripides? Of course, Ben Jon-
son knew Euripides, but I wonder whether such a
reference could possibly have been understood by
an Elizabethan audience.

CREECH. How do we know there *was* any such
audience?

SCENE VIII

*Placard: "Naples." Charles of Anjou and Lucia.
He is reading a letter which she has just brought
him.*

CHARLES.
Sacré bleu! Mille tonnerres! What news is this?
Perfidio, our man in Sicily,
Declares that a great rising of the island
Is toward—that Manfred's widow, Spanish
    Constance,
And some mad monk are lurking in Palermo
To plot our overthrow. *Comment diable!*
Sapristi! Ventre-Dieu! We must halt our plan—
We must postpone our expedition
To far Byzance, and swiftly to Messina
Unfold an instant and a secret sail!

LUCIA (*who has repressed her first signs of shock
and has been thinking very quickly. She speaks in
a cute little American voice, which contrasts with
her fell intentions*).
'Twere better then, my liege, to feign ill health,
Masking your absence—better not to breast
With your brave galleon's swollen wings the sea,
Nor ride at anchor with your retinue.
They must not know, the foul conspirators,
That thou hast privily received intelligence

51

Of their design. Harken, my liege, I know
A most adroit and trusty fisherman,
Who plies 'twixt Naples and Sicilian shores
And like a seabird floats nor fears rough weather.
He makes the passage often, oft conveys
Poor merchants. He is known in every port.
His comings and his goings are scarce noted.

    CHARLES.

Lucia, thou first camest to our Naples
A malapert and saucy serving maid,
Yet soon thou didst subdue our royal household—
Our Franks *dépaysés* in this foreign place—
To order strict and partial harmony
With sullen strangers, for thou dids't interpret,
Adept at both the tongues, for all our court,
And now, *parbleu, ma chère*, thou servest us
As our best prompter.

    LUCIA.

                Let me then, my liege,
Stay ever by your side, and go with you.
I have, besides, another anxious reason:
By this same messenger who brought to you
These tidings came a letter from Palermo
That bore the news my agèd mother there
Is dying and would see me ere she passes.
So I would seek Palermo and receive
Her final breath. Thus, all unspied upon,
I shall spy out what machinations
May be afoot against your Majesty.
For safety I may travel as your page,

So none shall know me when we do embark,
And you, my liege, I think, must don rude garments,
Like some poor trafficker in figs and dates.
An't please your Majesty, I'll straight to market
And fit you with a lading of these fruits,
As if I bought provision for the palace.
    CHARLES.
Dépêche-toi, donc, and waste no moment there!
Find also the false dress for me to wear.
    LUCIA.
I'll have the boat made ready.
    CHARLES.

                     Bon, allons!
Mort de ma vie, quelle situation!
    He hurries out.
    LUCIA.
So far, so good. Now comes the test of it,
The trial of my swift Sicilian wit,
To lead astray this dunce and dunderhead
And, with God's help, to leave the dizzard dead.

SCENE IX

Backstage during the intermission. Fran and Winslow.

FRAN (*nervous*). I'm sorry about that slip. It's been haunting me that way all through the rehearsals—I was afraid I was going to say it.

WINSLOW. It's all right. It made them laugh.

FRAN. Don't you think it might be a good idea to skip Terry's scene with you and Lucia. I'm sure he's had more drinks.

WINSLOW. I don't think he'll let us down.

FRAN. You love that scene with the Clown. It might have a scholar in stitches. But nobody who doesn't get the allusions and the Elizabethan vocabulary is going to understand a word of it.

WINSLOW. It's no more difficult than some of Shakespeare's clown scenes.

FRAN. That goes for Shakespeare, too. Either they cut them or they have to mug them.

WINSLOW. It's too late to leave it out. Don't worry, dear. It's going to be all right.—See if Lucia's ready.

He goes on stage. Fran is on her way to the door of a dressing room when Lucia emerges in her page costume.

FRAN. You're ready, little linnet?

*Chuck and Terry, together, come out of an-
other door laughing, and Terry goes on stage.*

FRAN (*to Chuck*). Have you been drinking, too?

CHUCK. Giovanni has to steel himself.

FRAN. Now don't actually beat Spooky up when
it comes to the duel scene!

CHUCK. Why not?

FRAN. You know you mustn't bully inferiors.

CHUCK. Inferiors? He's just had me fired.

FRAN. You know what I mean. You were saying
that you and he were on different levels. So don't.

The bell rings. The backstage goes dark.

SCENE X

Placard: "Palermo." The Duke sits looking at a miniature. Terry-Clown enters before he has finished his apostrophe to it.

WINSLOW-DUKE.
'Tis well, Ardelia, my sweet wife, that thou
Liv'st not to endure these dark and bloody days—
Thou who didst daunt the people with thy beauty,
Whom after years I still beheld with wonder
The sharer of my table and my bed.
Like any common shepherd, I was dazzled;
My pride itself did vail before thy pride.
These days, I say, are dark, yet every day
Is darkling since thou went'st. There is no dawn
For my sad spirit since its sun is gone.
    TERRY-CLOWN.
You are sad, my lord.
    WINSLOW-DUKE.

                    Say, where hast thou been hiding?
In some low stews, I'll warrant, some lewd tavern.
Beware our sly Cataines and cunning coles,
Crackhalters quick to cozen Northern gulls.
Thy master called for thee and thou cam'st not.
    TERRY CLOWN. I'faith, a man of the North who
hath scaped without a pox the bona robas of Turn-

bull-Street and the coney-catchers of Ram's Alley
hath nought to fear from the golls of your Southern
fingerers or the trulls of your Sicilian trugging-
houses. No haggard like a German haggard!

WINSLOW-DUKE (*to the audience*). A word of
explanation here. A haggard is one who resists a
cony-catcher. (*Continuing*) Thou boastest like a
very Teuton. Look to it that thou be'st not provoked in a coil with our Mafia hacksters.

TERRY-CLOWN.

Nay, for me provoked is prorogued.

WINSLOW-DUKE.

How so, knave?

TERRY-CLOWN.

I strive to appease the bully, and should the rogue
still provoke, eftsoons I prorogue again.

WINSLOW-DUKE.

Meantime, thou may'st catch a firking.

TERRY-CLOWN.

Nay, I'll find some pat firk to firk off.

WINSLOW-DUKE (*to the audience—he has been
thoroughly enjoying this dialogue*). Shakespeare
may have written this! *Firk* was a common Elizabethan word. It was used in several senses: as a
verb, it meant, to whip and to dart off; as a noun,
it could mean a trick, a dodge. You have all three
of these meanings here.—(*To the Clown*) What is
thy business, sirrah, now thou art come at last?

TERRY-CLOWN.

A young man to see you, my lord—though he hath

more the mien of a maid. He speaks our tongue,
yet I fear some mischief.

    WINSLOW-DUKE.

Bid him enter, and do thou stay by.

    Clown goes out.

    WINSLOW-DUKE (*putting aside the miniature*).

Ardelia, whom I trusted, my stanch bride,
Now must I fear deceit on every side.

    Clown enters with Lucia in her page's costume.

    LUCIA.

Mistake me not in this strange garb, my lord.

    WINSLOW-DUKE.

Lucia! Safe from Naples? Little linnet,
How dids't thou fly?

    LUCIA.

                I shipp'd with our good fisher,
And with a passenger that will astound
Your ears to hear on. Charles the Angevin
Hath, by his agent, one Perfidio,
Got wind of what is plotted. In disguise,
He hath joined his fleet that masses at Messina
And straight moves on Palermo, where he plans
To rout our patriots, after Easter vespers,
Fresh from their prayers and pious applications
Of bread and wine that, through our Saviour's
    blood,
Have purified their hearts—which shall be spitted
To shed their own; their throats that have voic'd
    God's anthem,
Shall now like those of squeaking swine be slit.

To frustrate this we must find means, my lord.
All seething Sicily awaits your word.

  WINSLOW-DUKE (*to Clown*).

Now, sirrah, babble not of this abroad.
Nay, we shall keep thee close.—I must take counsel
Of Prince Giovanni. Meantime, brave Lucia,
Stay here and see this rascal stray not forth
To gossip in the wine-shops.

  LUCIA.

        Ay, my lord.

 The Duke hurries out.

  TERRY-CLOWN.

They call thee "little linnet." Canst thou sing? This
Sicily hath nought but scrannel pipes and cater-
wauling fit only for the ears of goats.

  LUCIA.

I sing neither for goats nor knaves.

  TERRY-CLOWN.

I am an honest knave, forsooth.

  LUCIA.

And, forsooth, a sore ill-favored.

  TERRY-CLOWN.

Nay, Mistress Pert, I have bussed and culled better
than you.

  LUCIA.

My lord the Duke wants discretion. He should sink
thee deep in dungeon lest thou prate.

  TERRY-CLOWN.

If so, I'll do as Queen Eleanor. Sunk at Charing
Green, she rose again at Queenhithe.

LUCIA.

Your skin should have a sound swaddling.

TERRY-CLOWN.

My master loves me well, hath never swing'd me.
And mayhap you will love me, for I love a lass that
takes no teasing, but snap snap makes smart riposte.

LUCIA.

An almond for a parrot!

TERRY-CLOWN.

Woulds't thou lead apes in Hell then?

LUCIA.

Were I to play at barleybreak with you, I'd soon
find myself in Hell with a knave and a cungerhead.

TERRY-CLOWN.

Marry, she takes the wall and makes me walk i' the
kennel.

LUCIA.

Marry mew, marry muff, marry hang you, good-
man dog!

    *Enter Winslow-Duke with Giovanni and Con-
stance.*

WINSLOW-DUKE (*to the audience*). That scene
really belongs to the subplot, but I couldn't help
leaving it in. How Swinburne would have chortled
over it!

WINSLOW-DUKE.

Would, madam, thou hadst brought with thee from
    Spain
A basket of those poisonous Spanish figs
That first bring cramps, then a convulsèd death.

MRS. SIMMS-CONSTANCE (*producing one from her corsage*).
We always carry one about our person.
We never know what enemy may deserve
This sovran remedy.
    WINSLOW-DUKE.
               Take it, good Lucia,
And proffer it to the Angevin when the thirst
That will assail him in our streets adust
Demands assuagement. For I like it not,
My prince, the cruel means you have devis'd
To make him die in torment.
    CHUCK-GIOVANNI.
                Would I were
Phalaris, that old tyrant of your isle,
Who roasted culprits in a brazen bull,
Red-heated from a fire stok'd beneath it,
Whose roarings were the howls of burning sinners.
I can afford no bronze nor cunning sculptors,
But, having some skill at carpentry, have contriv'd
An engine to repress the Angevin
And make us mirthful with his mangled groans!
    WINSLOW-DUKE (*to Lucia*).
Try first the fig. I like not deeds of horror,
E'en when provok'd by horrors and deserv'd.

Wilt thou not sing, Lucia, to relieve
The heavy burdens of this somber house—
That old song that the Duchess lov'd. Alas.
'Twill make me sadder but my rancor pass.

LUCIA (*sings*).

When the south wind doth blow
    Beneath a leaden sky,
    We seek, my love and I,
A nook no man may know,
And there we clip and kiss.

When fading of the gale
    Unveils an azure sky,
    We sleep, my love and I,
Drows'd by the sun's dwale,
Yet wake to kiss and clip.

Might we forever kiss
    In shadow or in sun,
    The two that play at one,
Then were we wise, ywis,
To dwell and die like this.

WINSLOW-DUKE.
How sooth and plaintive-sweet this music falls!
She was want to sing it at her virginals.
—But now a long farewell to music's charms:
We face contention's strife and war's alarms.
    Trumpet.

TISDALE. "Drugged by the sun's dwale"?
CREECH. A soporific drink. Farfetched.

TISDALE. Did the Mafia exist in the Renaissance?
Creech, not knowing, does not reply. Tisdale glances at him.
TISDALE. One would have to check on that.
No reply.

SCENE XI

Placard: "A Street in Palermo." Charles and Lucia, still disguised.

LUCIA.

Put off a little still your kingly state,
My liege, to grace this humble merchant's garb.
Your guards, disguisèd, too, shall seek the church
Like harmless worshippers, and till the springe be
      sprung
Shew not yourself among the sullen people
Who, at your sight, might spew their hate like Etna.
But come to where your loyal followers,
Those of our people who defend the Franks,
Do wait to hear the trumpet of your tongue,
Be rous'd to ardor by your royal presence.
    (*Spooky-Perfidio slips in at the side and listens
    to the conversation.*)
They are gathered in the darkness of the crypt,
Where none dare enter, for they fear the dead
In that most dedicate and dreadful place.
    (*Producing the poisonous fig*)
A fig, my liege, to slake your parchèd throat,
In this our scorch'd and dusty Sicily?
    (*Aside*)
—I would not send him to a death so cruel.

64

I have borne so long I almost come to pity
His stout and obstinate stupidity.
    CHARLES.
A fortnight on the daz'd and queasy seas
I nothing eat but figs and dates.
    LUCIA.
                      I, too,
Did have a surfeit of this syrup'd fruit—
And when we came to port, I inly quak'd
Lest we be question'd, and our strategem
Discoverèd, since figs as futile are
To Sicily as pilchards fetch'd to Yarmouth.
—Come then, my liege, and softly through the
    streets
We'll make our cloakèd way.
    Churchbells.
    CHARLES.
                Lead on, sweet page,
Thou hast ever prov'd a torch, a star, to me.
Diantre! En avant! Ventre-saint-gris!
  They go out.
  SPOOKY-PERFIDIO.
I like not this. This page is too glib-lipp'd.
Needs must I glimpse what passes in the crypt.
    Perfidio follows Charles and Lucia.
    *A noble Sicilian and his wife appear, and at
the same time a Sergeant. During the scene that
follows, other men and women drift in, both
Sicilians and French.*

THE WIFE.
Sweet husband, what a winter do we face,
Sans grain, sans flesh of cattle or of swine.
Our mares and geldings they have rapp'd away
To ride against the Turks.
      THE HUSBAND.

                                    May the Turks mince them!
May the false Crescent of the infidel!
Cut down this beast that falsely bears the Cross,
As if a carrion raven did croak forth
He were the Holy Ghost!
      THE SERGEANT.

                                    These dogs of Dagoes,
This scum of Sicily, sometimes carry arms
To catch their masters in a *guet-apens*.
—Come, fellow, what hast thou hid beneath thy
      cloak?
      He searches the Husband.
      THE HUSBAND.
Lay off, thou swallower of frogs!
      THE SERGEANT.

                                    And thou, bold wench,
What hast thou in thy bodice?
      He puts his hand in her bosom.
      THE HUSBAND.

                                    Touch her not!
      *While the Sergeant is mishandling the Wife,
      the Husband snatches his sword.*
      THE HUSBAND.
By thine own sword be slain and sent to Hell!

He stabs the Sergeant, who falls dead.

THE HUSBAND (*to the crowd who have gathered*).

Enough of Frankish insolence! Have at them!

THE SICILIANS (*who begin fighting the French*).

Mordanu li Franchiski! Down with the filthy Frogs!

THE FRENCH.

Mort aux sales Siciliens! Down with the Dagoes!

A SICILIAN (*pointing to a woman*).

She lies with the Franks, this strumpet, and she hath a Froggish baby in her womb. Do her to death!

They set upon the woman.

ANOTHER SICILIAN.

They cannot speak, they lisp!

To a Frenchman, whom two other Sicilians are holding.

Say *céci*, knave!

THE FRENCHMAN.

Sesí, sesí.

The French all try to pronounce the word and fail. The Sicilians slay them and chase them out.

The curtain descends, and while the scene is being changed, Winslow comes before it.

WINSLOW. I find that this part is historical. Although our author does at times take liberties, these horrors were entirely real. Today they ought not to surprise us. The language issue in Sicily—was most acute. It became a national grievance. And this ought not to surprise us either.

SCENE XII

Placard: "The Crypt."

The crypt, on the left, has a spiral stair. A black catafalque with a coffin on top; the draperies reach to the ground. The Duke, Constance, Violante and the Clown stand around in black dominoes with hoods. Giovanni, in his Friar's gown, presides. All are chanting as Charles and Lucia enter right.

LUCIA (*to Charles*).
They do but play at obsequies and dirges.
The coffin's empty, and the hooded friar
Hath rallied here your faithful followers.
CHUCK-GIOVANNI (*seeing them*).
Seize him! Disarm him! Clown, do thou bar the door!
Look you, it is the Angevin!
CHARLES

Zut, alors!
Terry-Clown locks the door, then he, the Duke and Queen Constance lay hands on Charles and take away his sword.
CHUCK-GIOVANNI.
And I the son of Conradin, dread sir—Giovanni of Procida!
(*Producing the Crowned Skull*)

See how my father, wearing still the crown,
Doth ghastly glare and grin on his destroyer!
> *The curtains of the inner stage open and reveal the Skeletons.*

Behold his court who muster to avenge him!

THE SKELETONS.

Avenge! Avenge! Avenge!

CHUCK-GIOVANNI.

Nay, give the boorish princeling back his sword.
'Tis I must fit him—I in single combat!
I'll slash and drag him to his spikèd coffin.

FRAN-VIOLANTE.

Ah, jeopard not thy noble spirit, prince,
With odds of such a heavy adversary!
We shall dispatch him as we first prepared.
Were we to lose thee, we should leaderless
Be left. Thou lit'st our flame to fight dishonor.
Our tears could never wash away such woe!

CHUCK-GIOVANNI.

Nay, loyal Violante, my quick blade,
Well-school'd in glitt'ring play, shall featly pierce
And slice and barbecue this lumbering ox!
Else were it treason to my father's name.
—Give back his sword.

> *The Duke returns it. In the meantime, without being noticed, Perfidio has crept down by the spiral stair.*

Now, Charles the Dog, have
at you!

> *They fight. Giovanni still holding the Skull*

under his left arm. Giovanni has the advantage,
but when he has driven Charles into the corner
where Perfidio is lurking, the latter trips up Gio-
vanni, and he falls upon Charles's sword.
CHUCK-GIOVANNI.

Brought low by base Perfidio, the spy,
Undone by unassuagèd pride, I die.
Good Duke, sweet Violante, to whom, dead,
I'll never, as we vainly hop'd, be wed:
Thou livest; to our lofty mission look:
See that this monstrous frog scape not the hook.

> *Violante kneels beside him.*
> *The Skeletons rush up behind Charles and hold*
> *him. The Duke and the Clown wrest away his*
> *sword.*

MRS. SIMMS-CONSTANCE.

A coffin for the tyrant: load him in.
TERRY-CLOWN.

Like Nürnberg's Iron Maiden, the grim coffin
Is lin'd with ravenous fangs.

> *The Skeletons open the lid, which is seen to be*
> *studded with long spikes. The others carry*
> *Charles to the coffin.*

CHARLES.

Unhand me, goblins, Devil's brood! *Morbleu!*
What make you in God's temple, *nom de Dieu?*
THE SKELETONS.

Avenge! Avenge! Avenge!

> *While they are putting him into the coffin and*
> *closing the lid, Perfidio turns to sneak up the*

*stair. Giovanni partly rises and, tackling him as
at football, brings him down. For this purpose,
he has to drop the Skull. Terry-Clown swiftly
picks it up and, holding it under his arm like a
football, plunges across the stage and makes a
touchdown on the other side.*

TERRY-CLOWN.

Touchdown for Hillsdale! Hillsdale 13, Middlebury
9!

THE SKELETONS (*led by Terry*).

Hillsdale! Hillsdale! Hillsdale! Avenge! Avenge!
Avenge!

CHUCK-GIOVANNI.

Let vile Perfidio feel those splinters' sting!
Impact him in the coffin with the King!

The Skeletons seize Perfidio, who struggles.

MRS. SIMMS (*coming out of her role*).

What's going on here? I won't put up with this!

She tries to intervene.

TERRY-CLOWN.

Take her away and have her soundly firked!

*Two of the Skeletons grip her arms and make
as if to escort her out. Winslow tries to go to her
rescue. She slaps away their hands.*

WINSLOW (*to the Skeletons*).

Please don't!

*In the meantime, the other Skeletons have been
cramming Perfidio into the coffin. They fasten
the lid and sit on it. One, however, abstains and
stands aside.*

Terry starts a football song, in which the Skeletons join.

So hit the line for Hillsdale,
For Hillsdale wins today!
And the Middlebury team will tremble
When they see the red and gray!

TERRY-CLOWN.

Now, boys, all together. Avenge! Avenge! Avenge!

THE SKELETONS.

Avenge! Avenge! Avenge!

TERRY-CLOWN.

Go, bid the soldiers shoot!

WINSLOW.

Please, please!

He makes gestures to quiet them. Perfidio and Charles, who have landed on a mattress below the coffin and have come out through the open side of the catafalque, now appear from behind it.

TERRY-CLOWN.

The monsters are loose again!

WINSLOW-DUKE (*to Charles and Perfidio*).

Please pretend to be dead.

CHARLES.

Things are getting out of hand.

SPOOKY-PERFIDIO.

Hadn't you better ring the curtain down?

WINSLOW-DUKE.

If you'd just lie down again.

SPOOKY-PERFIDIO.

I don't think you can handle it.

FRAN (*to Chuck*).
Do something!

CHUCK-GIOVANNI (*who is sitting up*).
Lay off, Skeletons. Can it, Terry. If Perfidio and
Charles will be dead, I'll be dead, too. Come on,
we'll all be dead.

WINSLOW-DUKE.
Yes: let us finish the play. *Please.* (*To the audience.*)
I'm sorry for this disturbance.

> *Giovanni falls dead with a percussive flop. Per-
> fidio and Charles subside behind the catafalque.*

FRAN-VIOLANTE (*going into her mad scene*).
Ah, uncle, see, how like a knight he lies
In marble on some brave crusader's tomb.
And I in the next compartment.

> (*She stretches out beside Giovanni.*)

                                        Now my flesh
To marble freezes. Now the footsteps pass
Above the pavement stone—and we are stone.
We hear mass chanted, supine, side by side.
Eternity drips on. Our passion passes,
Leaving us pale and numb. Ah, never more
To dance i' the spring. Our limbs are turn'd to
    marble.
We lie forever in death's long defeat.

WINSLOW-DUKE.
Defeat, defeat. My child, defeat is sure.
Giovanni lost, our cause is lost. Farewell,
Dear niece. Farewell to life. Thou'rt mad, and I

Weighed down with the sad impotence of eld
That cannot keep what once my dukedom held.

    He stabs her, then stabs himself. Shouts are
    heard from outside. The Duke, tottering, opens
    the door. A Sicilian comes running up.

    THE SICILIAN.

The Duke! Oh, my good lord, the people have risen!
They storm the market-place and put to the sword
Those lispers who speak not our rugged tongue.
Their Charles was here, but now, they say, is mur-
    dered!

    WINSLOW-DUKE (*sinking down*).

Pray God, they conquer! I am old, and I
Can only, never acquiesce, but die.

    He dies.

    THE SICILIAN (*taking off his hat and standing*
    beside the Duke).

There snapped the strings that tuned the martial
    song.
The song for ever lasts; the lute not long.
Now set him where the saints and soldiers are.
The gold of fame outglows the wrack of war.

SCENE XIII

Winslow comes before the curtain.

WINSLOW. And now, before delivering the Epilogue, I should like to invite my distinguished col-
league, Dr. Edgar J. Creech of Pratt College—perhaps at present the world's leading authority on the
texts of the Elizabethan drama—who has honored us
with his presence here tonight—to favor us with a
few words on his impressions of the play which we
have just performed. I am sure that Dr. Creech understands that what I fear I must call the monkey-
shines in the final scene were not a part of the actual
script and represented a perhaps pardonable injec-
tion of undergraduate high spirits. Our actors, in
their riotous behavior, had, in fact, I think, caught
something of the spirit of the roistering Elizabethans.—Dr. Creech, would you care to give an opinion—on the possible provenience of the play?

CREECH (*rising*). I don't need to make any allowances for the alleged interpolations of the actors in
order to give a verdict on this ridiculous charade.
The so-called text of the play is no more authentic
than these interpolations. The thing is a forgery
from beginning to end. It is necessary only to indi-
cate that—among the many outrageous absurdities
—the word *Dago,* derived from the Spanish name

75

Diego, originated in the United States sometime
early in the nineteenth century, and that the word
Frog in the Elizabethan period meant a Dutchman
not a Frenchman. (*Winslow smiles.*) To try to
make us accept such balderdash is, on somebody's
part, a barefaced piece of impudence. (*He sits
down.*)

WINSLOW. Thank you, Dr. Creech, for your
frank opinion. And now for our Epilogue:

My lords and ladies, may you be disposed
My fault to pardon if I have imposed
On your credulity—if believe you did:
I've sometimes thought that there was nothing hid
From some sharp wits—such as Dr. Creech's, for
          example—and yet some did incline
To take for Chettle's what was really mine.
For Shakespeare—pray forgive the blasphemy—
I hoped—no doubt, deludedly—to see
Some words of mine for his to be mistaken,
Though audience and author must awaken
To recognize that I, poor fool, was fakin';
To know such lines no living hand may trace
Now that the master's multifeatured face,
Behind which hides the man, may never wear
Another avatar, grotesque or fair,
Of murderer or maiden, lord or loon.
And yet we may renew that music's tune.
We needs must live the poets that we cherish;
We needs must tend their spirits lest they perish—

Not peer at them from scholarly removes:
Each man perhaps must forge the book he loves.
To challenge Chettle though I may aspire,
With Shakespeare's genius I can aim no higher
Than dimly to communicate, forsooth,
Some spark of splendor to our groping youth,
And few have I found so dull they could not thrill
To some live facet of that genius still.
—Forgive my brief deception, do not grudge
My self-indulgence in a dream, nor judge
Too strictly the poor tribute that I pay
To an age that, though long gone, can never pass
away.
—My lords and ladies, deeply thankèd be.
To our actors pray accord your plaudité.
*The curtain goes up, and the actors take their
bows.*

TISDALE (*to Creech, as they are putting on their
coats*). We're invited to a reception at Winslow's
house.

CREECH. I shan't go.

TISDALE. I'll say you are rather fatigued.

CREECH. I am *not* fatigued at all. I don't want to
consort with that clown.

TISDALE. Since I'm destined to be a mountebank,
I might as well consort with mountebanks. And I
don't think he's wholly unsympathetic. They say
he was unhinged by the death of his wife.

CREECH. A scholar should never marry: it breaks up his application to his work. Children! Bills! Automobiles! I had a married brother. He's dead. It was the best he could hope for.

They walk across the stage and go out at the left, Creech stalking ahead.

INTERMISSION

SCENE XIV

The Winslow living room. On a table, whisky, soda and glasses. Winslow and Fran come back from the theater.

FRAN. I skipped the first part of the mad scene because I knew at that point they'd just laugh.

WINSLOW. I don't know. It was a pity to lose it.

FRAN. I suspected you might have written the play yourself, but I never paid enough attention to see that you'd put everybody into it.

WINSLOW. Don't say anything about that aspect. I doubt whether anyone's guessed.

FRAN. You let them disqualify Winky Carter on purpose so that Chuck could play Giovanni?

WINSLOW. No: that was more or less of an accident.—That must be the phone.

FRAN. No, it isn't. You're so evasive. You always pretend to hear the phone.—What did you mean by the French occupation?

WINSLOW.
I've felt them closing in. They do not speak our
    tongue.
I've felt our home has quite become a prison,
Whence soon we scarce shall dare to stir abroad.
They seek to stifle me, to clip the wings
Of Pegasus, to blind Apollo's radiance.

FRAN. Oh, come! It's not as bad as that. And
we've had enough blank verse tonight.—But you
held them right up to the end.

WINSLOW. The castle of Conradin might be the
palace of literature, in which the knights have been
turned into skeletons.

FRAN. The part about Mother was touching.

WINSLOW. I wrote that little lyric that Lucia
sings when your Mother and I were in Sicily.—It's
a good thing she *wasn't* there tonight. She'd have
seen me make a fool of myself.

*He sits down and, as if on the verge of weep-
ing, covers his face with his hands.*

FRAN. Oh, no: you carried it off splendidly.

WINSLOW (*beginning to laugh and becoming
more and more hysterical*). Terry and Mrs. Simms!
Creech coming all the way from California!

FRAN. What a nasty old character! But the joke
is on him. Why did you put in the Frogs and the
Dagoes?

WINSLOW. I couldn't resist it. Ha, ha! I wanted
to see whether they'd notice. (*He cannot curb his
fou rire.*) Charley Patterson's French! I wrote it
especially for him.

FRAN. I didn't know you disliked Charley Patterson so much.

WINSLOW. I don't but he's such a dolt to be President of a college—and he'll never have the least
suspicion.

FRAN. It's been a strain tonight. You better have a drink before people come.

She pours him one and gives it to him. The doorbell rings. Fran goes to answer it.

WINSLOW. That must be the telephone!

Wiping his eyes, he hurries away into the study. Fran brings in Warren Tisdale and Mr. and Mrs. Patterson. Patterson, who has played Charles d'Anjou, is a big burly goodnatured man.

FRAN (*to Tisdale*). This is President and Mrs. Patterson. Mr. Tisdale—of Pratt College in California.

PATTERSON. Oh, I know Mr. Tisdale. We met at an MLA conference.

TISDALE. Yes, of course.

PATTERSON. You were one of the shining lights.

TISDALE. Oh, hardly.

PATTERSON. I tried to tempt you to Hillsdale.

Winslow comes back from the study.

WINSLOW. Hello, Charley! Hello, Mamie! Delighted to see you, Dr. Tisdale.

TISDALE. It was great fun tonight.

MRS. PATTERSON. You're so clever, Homer! I thought it was genuine right up to the end.

WINSLOW. I'm sorry it ran off the tracks. You were tremendous, Charley—a thousand thanks for playing that part! It was very sporting of you!

PATTERSON. I was a little bit surprised when Ned Simms was dumped on top of me.

WINSLOW. That wasn't on the program, of course. I didn't mean you to get such rough treatment.

PATTERSON. Oh, I've never stood on my dignity. And I used to play football myself, you know. (*He laughs.*) I was glad to hear their outburst of college spirit.

The doorbell rings, and Fran starts to go.

WINSLOW. Take them into the dining room, Fran.

FRAN. Don't you want a snack, Mr. Tisdale. You can't have had time for dinner.

TISDALE. I've only had a very inferior sandwich. Yes, I should. Thank you.

They go out into the hall.

PATTERSON. Could I have a word with you, Homer?

WINSLOW. Certainly.

PATTERSON. Something rather alarming has broken about Ned Simms. Is he here?

WINSLOW. No: he hasn't come yet.

PATTERSON. You know that East Mansfield motel that already has a bad reputation? Well, the Chief of Police came to see me today and told me that they're going to clean it up. He told me to warn Ned Simms. He was very frank and decent about it and said that he didn't want anybody from the College involved. But if I speak to Ned about it, I really can't let him stay on. That's one thing I can't stand for. We had a scandal here six years ago, when the Fine Arts man used to have the bootblack from the barbershop come to his rooms for tea—so of course I had to get rid of him.

WINSLOW. I suspected something of the kind, but I've always believed in tolerance.

PATTERSON. I can't afford to be tolerant. The trustees might hear about it, and I'd better act right away.

WINSLOW. He's got tenure.

PATTERSON. This overrules tenure.

WINSLOW (*thoughtfully*). Yes: James the First was a notorious homosexual, and it was during the reign of James that the English drama ran to seed. I never could like Beaumont and Fletcher.—But of course there was the King James Bible.

PATTERSON. The police have got plenty on him, and I think I'll have to put it to him frankly. Besides, I don't like his influence—I've been to some of his lectures, and they seem to me very farfetched. And if there's going to be a vacancy, it's occurred to me tonight that we might get Warren Tisdale. I heard him read a paper at the MLA on the Gothic influence on Poe. I hadn't known about that before. I thought it was a crackerjack. I've been thinking of sounding him out tonight.

WINSLOW. I'm afraid you're going to find that you can't get him away from Creech. He expects to be his successor.

Some of the guests begin drifting in, with glasses and plates in their hands: among them, Warren Tisdale, who is chatting urbanely with

Lucia; and a beatnikish-looking young man with a beard.

THE YOUNG MAN. Professor Winslow, I'm Ronald Pfeiffer, an off-Broadway producer from New York: the Baroque Players. You've probably never heard of them.

WINSLOW. Oh, yes, I have. They put on *The Honest Whore.*

PFEIFFER. Did you see it?

WINSLOW. Yes, I did. I thought it a very creditable production!

PFEIFFER. I must say it was an unexpected success. There's a public for the plays of that period. And what I want to tell you is how ardently I congratulate you on your marvellous play tonight. There's nothing I'd like so much as to have our theater do it.

WINSLOW. Of course, you must understand that the last scene was somewhat messed up.

PFEIFFER. I wouldn't change a word of it! I'd want to do it just as it was done tonight. It combines the neo-baroque with the theater of the absurd.

WINSLOW (*very much pleased*). Well, we might talk about it.

Pfeiffer and Winslow continue their conversation, while Patterson brings Tisdale to the front of the stage, and they sit down to talk in a corner. Lucia is now engaged with two of the football-playing Skeletons. A pansy English instructor has drifted in alone and while quietly eating his salad and ham listens in on the following conversation.

PATTERSON. You remember that several years ago I tried to get you to come to Hillsdale. We weren't able to offer you as much then as we can now since we've got a foundation grant. But I'm afraid you're indispensable to Dr. Creech.

TISDALE. Oh, no: not necessarily.

PATTERSON. Well, there's a distinct possibility that Ned Simms may have to hand in his resignation. New England isn't good for his asthma, and he really needs a drier climate. The idea has just occurred to me that we might effect an exchange?

TISDALE. For Simms to go out to Pratt? I should think it might be arranged. They've been wanting an explication man out there. They think I'm an old romantic. And I'd be very glad indeed to get back to the East again. I've never really adapted myself to California: a certain goodnatured emptiness—I don't speak of Dr. Creech.

PATTERSON. That's splendid! I'll talk to Ned Simms. (*He gets up.*) Could you stay over another day?

TISDALE (*as they walk away from the corner*). Yes, certainly.

Patterson. Then come to my office in the afternoon. I'll call you up in the morning.

Their voices are lost among the general conversation, and we hear the voices of Winslow and Pfeiffer.

PFEIFFER. Would it be possible anywhere in New York to get one's beard trimmed like that?

WINSLOW. I always go to Henri at the Vanderbilt-Plaza.

PFEIFFER. That's a fine job he's done on you—distinguished and chic. I think that, as a baroque producer, I ought to look more seventeenth century. These beatnik beavers are quite old hat.

Spooky Simms comes in with a drink. The Pansy Instructor takes him by the arm and steers him toward the front of the stage. A non-football-playing Skeleton comes up to him on the way.

SKELETON. I wanted to tell you, sir, that I didn't take part in the roughhouse. I'm grateful for the B-minus you gave me on my paper about the graveyard symbolism in *Paul Revere's Ride.*

SPOOKY. But you missed the significance of the lanterns.

SKELETON. I'll try to do better, sir.

SPOOKY. All right, Wethey. (*He walks on.*)

PANSY. Mr. Patterson says you think of leaving.

SPOOKY. What?

PANSY. I heard him offering your job to Tisdale.

SPOOKY. Offering my job to Tisdale?

PANSY. Yes: he evidently wants to get rid of you.

SPOOKY. That fatuous old figurehead—he can't. What do you mean? I've got tenure.

PANSY. I'm afraid there's only one explanation. I told you that they watched that motel, and it seems they're about to close it.

SPOOKY. I only went there two or three times—

PANSY. Now, now!

SPOOKY. And that was a long time ago. He can't do it!

PANSY. He can tell you you'll have to resign or otherwise there'd be a scandal. The idea seems to be that you're to take Tisdale's job on the Coast. You wouldn't be getting so much, but I should think it would have its advantages. They say they're more permissive out there—it's less puritanical than New England—it's not far from San Francisco.

SPOOKY. But that side of my life is finished.

PANSY. I've always thought it was *utter madness* for you to think of marrying Fran Winslow. How would she get along with your mother—to say *nothing* of *other* considerations!

SPOOKY. You want to get rid of me, too, and I brought you here in the first place.

PANSY. Well, I've never been an explications man really, and you drive us with such a tight rein. I do think that an English Department ought to pay *some attention* to *literature as such!* I know that if I teach them to appreciate Keats, I'll never never get tenure!

Spooky walks away. Pansy looks after him with catty malice.

MRS. PATTERSON (*to Spooky*). You had such a difficult part! I hope that that fall didn't hurt you.

SPOOKY (*with a sour look*). Not at all.

A lean and eager young man comes in from the hall and goes up to Winslow.

YOUNG MAN. Are you Professor Winslow?

WINSLOW. Yes.

YOUNG MAN. I'm sorry to barge in uninvited like this, but nobody answered the bell, and I was told that Chuck Chambers was here. I've got something so important to tell him that I think really—warrants this rudeness.

WINSLOW. Certainly.

Chuck, hearing his name, appears from the study.

YOUNG MAN. Oh, there he is! Hello, Chuck. I've got sensational news! Will you excuse us for a moment, sir? (*They come to the front of the stage.*) There's a revolution at Harvard!

CHUCK (*morosely interrogative*). ?

YOUNG MAN. Ted Meyer's been made President.

CHUCK. That instructor who lost his job for writing those comic songs?

YOUNG MAN. Yes.

CHUCK. You're kidding.

YOUNG MAN. Oh, Ted is an astute character. In his songs he's insulted everybody: the Catholics, the Jews, the Negroes, the Civil Rights protesters, the hipsters, the scholars, the snobs. That guarantees impartiality. The young people think he's terrific.

CHUCK. How did he get by the Overseers?

YOUNG MAN. Oh, the Overseers aren't important. It's the Corporation—and there are only six of them. Two are in MacLean's Sanitarium; two are on LSD;

old Parker Bowditch is in his second childhood and thinks he's a liberal again, and Forbes Peabody is even farther gone—he thinks it's a question of freeing the slaves. And then there's the new Student Council that votes with the Corporation.

CHUCK. I didn't know about that.

YOUNG MAN. Oh, yes. The students, that time they demonstrated, demanded a voice in administration. Harvard has now an ambition to be known as the Berkeley of the East. You know there's been a policy from a long time back of getting it away from the Ivy League and giving it an overall national coverage.

CHUCK. Does Ted Meyer use phrases like that?

YOUNG MAN. No, but he says "uh-huh" when other people use them.

CHUCK. It won't last. The alumni won't stand for it.

YOUNG MAN. Of course, there's been a lot of protest, but they can't go against the Corporation, and Ted is very strong for athletics. He's made fun of that, too, but now he promises to make Harvard tops in football again. The people who take football seriously can't bear to have Dartmouth ahead of us, and Ted's giving scholarships to near-pro's. Half the faculty have resigned, and almost the whole of the Classics Department, and that's where *you* come in. They want you to come back and teach Greek.

CHUCK. I haven't got a Ph.D., and my discipline, as they say, is English.

YOUNG MAN. That's one of the great innovations. Ted has made a revolutionary ruling that no new man is to be taken on who *has* got a Ph.D. He thinks that it destroys the intellect. And no more "publish or perish." Anybody who publishes a book has to have a commercial contract.

CHUCK. What about the University Press?

YOUNG MAN. It's going to print nothing but school bulletins, bulletins for the students at different ages and bulletins to teach the teachers how to teach the bulletins. So it will make a lot more money. (*The guests have been seen leaving, and Fran, who has been saying good-by to them, now comes back from the hall and listens to this conversation.*) Do come! You ought to jump at it. I know you're not at home here.

CHUCK. I'm not at home anywhere.

FRAN. What's this?

CHUCK. Believe it or not, he wants me to come to Harvard and teach in the Classics Department.

FRAN. I don't believe it. (*To Young Man*) I'm Professor Winslow's daughter.

CHUCK. I didn't believe it either. (*To Young Man*) Are you sure you're not full of LSD yourself?

YOUNG MAN. Nothing stronger than pot. If you've got any doubts about it, here's a letter from Ted himself.

CHUCK (*taking the letter and looking at it*). "Office of the President." Well, I'll be damned!

Young Man. Think it over and let me know to-morrow. I'm staying at the Old Red Coach House.

While Chuck is reading the letter, the Young Man takes his leave and goes.

Fran. What's happened at Harvard?

Chuck. It's incredible, but things do sometimes blow up nowadays. I suppose people think that if *they're* going to be blown up, they might as well blow up something first.

Fran. You'd better accept.

Chuck. It's possible.—You come along with me.

Fran. As nursemaid and mistress for you?

Chuck. Why do you want to play the old-fashioned girl?

Fran. Somebody's got to—

Chuck.—keep up standards.

Fran. Exactly.

Chuck. It's that thing you've got about your mother.

Fran. Perhaps.

Chuck. Well, let's get married, Fran. Let's get the hell out of Hillsdale!

Fran. I'm not going to push a baby-carriage around Cambridge.

Chuck. Who wants you to? Haven't you heard about the new technological improvements?

Fran. The first technological improvement for you will be to master the use of the razor—and a few other toilet accessories.

CHUCK. Well, I won't wear tweeds, I'll tell you, and I'm not going to smoke a pipe.

FRAN. And I suppose I take a graduate course at Radcliffe.

CHUCK. You'd have plenty to do helping me. And you wouldn't have to bother with faculty wives the way you do here.

FRAN. You don't know a college community.

CHUCK. I don't care about social life.

FRAN. Yes: you'd probably never let me see anybody.

CHUCK. This sounds like Millamant and Mirabell.

FRAN. I don't see where Mirabell comes in.— Besides, I can't leave Father.

CHUCK. We'll get him a job at Harvard—if so many jobs are going begging. It seems half the faculty's resigned.

Winslow comes in from the hall.

FRAN. Go home now. Father's tired, and I'm tired.

CHUCK. I'm never tired.

FRAN. I know it, but go home just the same.

She kisses him.

CHUCK (*to Winslow*). Good night, Duke. She's driving me out. "And flights of angels sing thee to thy rest."

WINSLOW. Good night, Chuck. I can't thank you enough for pinch-hitting at the last moment! And you gave such a splendid performance! You were really the best thing in the play—though you were a little rough with Ned Simms. Poor fellow, he's got his own cross to bear.

CHUCK.
The devil damn him black, the cream-fac'd loon!
Where got he that goos'd look?

Winslow laughs goodnaturedly. Chuck leaves.

FRAN. That friend of Chuck's who was here says there's been a revolution at Harvard. Half the faculty have resigned, and they want Chuck for the Classics Department.

WINSLOW. A good idea, but rather abnormal.

FRAN. Well, everything that's happening nowadays is abnormal from the point of view of *your* generation. But ours can't be bothered to be surprised. We have to be ready to take anything on.

WINSLOW. And Chuck's going to take this on?

FRAN. I think so.

WINSLOW. Well, anything of the kind is certainly unprecedented for Harvard!

FRAN. What's even more unprecedented is that he's just asked me to marry him.

WINSLOW. How are you going to deal with that? Don't be too brutal about it.

FRAN. I haven't made up my mind.

WINSLOW. You don't mean you're seriously considering it?

FRAN. I might.

WINSLOW. You mustn't get married now.

FRAN. Not until after I graduate and Chuck is sure of his job.

WINSLOW. Do you think you'd be happy with Chuck?

FRAN. He needs somebody to take him in charge,

and I've already been working at that here. If he's
left to himself at Harvard, he may simply make
himself impossible even with this new regime.

WINSLOW. He's certainly very rebarbative.

FRAN. You're going to say, once a sorehead always
a sorehead.

WINSLOW. No, I wasn't. Not necessarily. But
Chuck is so hopelessly anti-social that it's hard to
imagine him giving you a life that would—be satis-
factory to you.

FRAN. I thought you believed in his abilities.

WINSLOW. I certainly think him brilliant—the
most extraordinary man, perhaps, that we've ever
had here at Hillsdale. I'm not sure he's not a genius.
But—

FRAN. I know that it's a kind of excavation job,
but I like to work at tough assignments.

WINSLOW. Don't take it on just as a challenge.

FRAN. Why did you write those scenes if you
weren't thinking of Chuck and me?

WINSLOW. You and Chuck never entered my
head.

FRAN. They must have come out of your subconscious.

WINSLOW. The subconscious! Since Freud, it's
been overdone.—Are you sure you're being realistic?

FRAN (*laughing*). You're the last person in the
world to talk about not being realistic.—And what
about you and Mother?

Winslow. That was more or less different.

Fran. Is it true that she died of Hillsdale?

Winslow. No, of course, not. She wasn't always happy here, but she'd just had that operation.

Fran. Well, I know the academic racket, and I wouldn't wilt away at Harvard.

Winslow. Understand then I don't necessarily approve.

Fran. I don't want to hurt your feelings, but I can't go on forever keeping house for you here. You could come to Cambridge with us. They say there are any number of vacancies.

Winslow. They wouldn't want an old barn-stormer like me.

Fran. You could write some more plays. After all, there's always Mother's money.

Winslow. I don't like to think how your mother would feel about your marrying Chuck.

Fran. You can't actually stab me, Father. And you do make the Sicilians win. Chuck may turn out to be a big Sicilian and live to avenge our wrongs.

Winslow. There's the phone!

He hurries out.

Fran (*looking after him*). The phone didn't ring.

Terry (*before the curtain*).
Will Fran someday be Chuck's unblushing bride?
—The rest of us are all quite satisfied.
Creech has made sure that no one will succeed him;

Shakespeare is sure that Winslow's class will read
    him.
Tisdale is happy to come East to stay,
And Winslow will be acted off Broadway.
The President will find himself less taxed,
And Spooky find a climate more relaxed.
Chuck will be free at last to work at Greek,
Escaping, in conditions quite unique,
From academic mayhem, hate and rapine,
At Harvard, where such horrors never happen.
—But will our Fran for him true love confess?
Or, if they marry, will it be a mess?
Ah, that, my friends, is anybody's guess.

Elizabethan Song

Music by
Ira Mendlowitz
(c. 1570-1612)

When the south wind doth blow___ Be-neath a lead-en sky,___ We seek my love...and I, A nook no man may know,___ And there we clip and kiss. When fa-ding of the gale___ un-veils an a-zure sky,___ We sleep my love and

DR. McGRATH

1967

Dr. Charles McGrath's study. At stage right is the Doctor's desk, which looks like that of a business executive. An easy chair for visitors faces it at an angle to the audience, so that anybody sitting in it can be seen three-quarters face. Very far to stage left is a closed door. The back wall is lined with bookcases, containing, on the right, darkly bound theological works and, to the left, contemporary books, mostly with their dust jackets still on. Above these bookcases, leaning against the wall, are photographs of energetic modern divines whom Dr. McGrath admires and old prints of leaders of the Reformation. The wall on the left is bare, but has a window with old-fashioned square panes. Several of these panes have been broken as well as part of the frame between them, as if by a heavy stoning.

Dr. McGrath is sitting at his desk, with an open Bible before him. He is a powerful-looking man in his forties, but nervous and evidently suffering from some severe tension.

McGrath (*to himself, reading from Matthew 24*). "Watch therefore: for ye know not what hour your Lord doth come."

"But know this, that if the good man of the house had known in what watch the thief would come (*he looks up toward the door*) he would have watched, and would not have suffered his house to be broken up." (*He looks toward the window.*)

"Therefore be ye also ready: for in such an hour as ye think not the Son of Man cometh"—

A knock at the door. McGrath looks up startled.

McGrath. Yes?

A Servant enters. He is a slim, pale young man, with a pointed beard.

The Servant. There's a Mr. Duquesne to see you, Doctor.

McGrath. Oh, yes. Ask him to come in here.

The Servant goes out. McGrath puts a marker in the Bible and sets it aside; then rather ostentatiously begins to write.

Francis Duquesne comes in. He has the look of a distinguished scholar, thin and sallow and dry, and he speaks with a faint French accent. He has left his hat and coat outside. McGrath gets up and shakes hands with him from behind the desk.

Duquesne (*nodding toward the manuscript on the desk*). Another sizzling sermon?

McGrath. Sit down: I wanted to talk to you.

Duquesne (*sitting down in the easy chair*). Well, it's ages since I've seen you, Charley, though we're almost neighbors. The last thing I heard about you was that you were going to Allensburg,

Pennsylvania. The First Presbyterian Church, wasn't it?

McGrath. That didn't go through.

Duquesne. What a pity.

McGrath. It's been a severe disappointment.

Duquesne. What was the trouble?

McGrath. I'm not quite sure. I preached out there in October, and I know that I was very much wanted by the better elements in the congregation. I suspect that the Communists prevented it.

Duquesne. The Communists? In the congregation?

McGrath. Yes.

Duquesne. Do the Communists out there go to church?

McGrath. You never can tell nowadays. There are members of that congregation—even fairly well-to-do people—who refer to themselves as "liberals." When I hear the word *liberal* now, I know there are Communists around.

Duquesne. All the liberals aren't by any means Communists. I suppose I'm a liberal myself. And, Charley, I must say that any liberal might naturally be expected to object to the kind of sermons you've been preaching.

McGrath. I haven't seen you in church.

Duquesne. I read about them in the papers. You're getting a lot of publicity.

McGrath. Yes: I let the Communists have it. I haven't pulled any punches. In such a soft-headed

community as this—where they don't want to admit they're menaced—I'm bound to attract attention.

DUQUESNE. Where do you see the menace?

MCGRATH. Are you one of the softies, too? Don't
you know that the Copperworkers' Union is Communist from top to bottom?

DUQUESNE. What's your evidence for that?

MCGRATH. Their defiant attitude—the outrageous demands they're making!

DUQUESNE. All unions make demands. They
don't have to be Communists for that. Do you object on principle to organized labor?

MCGRATH. I've never known any good to come
of it.

DUQUESNE. They often get better conditions.

MCGRATH. At the cost of being ruled by the
Communists, and they're made to turn their backs
on religion.

DUQUESNE. A good many of these workers here
are Catholics—Italians and Poles and so on. There
are two Catholic churches in town, and both, I
understand, are well filled.

MCGRATH. That means that those Polacks and
Wops are enslaved to the Catholic Church.

DUQUESNE. To both Communism and the Catholic Church?

MCGRATH. You have two conspiracies at work.
I think they've made a deal with one another. I
give the Catholics a blast, too, from time to time.

DUQUESNE. Of course, you know that the Catholic policy now is to promote more cordial relations with the various Protestant churches.

McGRATH. They're trying to take us over. I believe that the Communists are behind the whole thing. Didn't Father Leary here come out for the copper-workers in the last strike? Didn't Khrushchyov go to see the Pope?

DUQUESNE. That was his son-in-law.

McGRATH. It's the same thing.

DUQUESNE. Look here, Charley: it may be that those elders in Allensburg—impressive, of course, though your sermons are—decided that you sometimes talked a little wildly.

McGRATH. That's always the accusation against a sincere reformer.

DUQUESNE. Well, people don't always want such alarming invectives as you've been giving them lately. They go to church to be edified and reassured.

McGRATH. What I want to do is wake them up.

DUQUESNE. You want to make them unsure and uncomfortable the way the old preachers did, with their visions of damnation, of being roasted alive for eternity—when ministers like Jonathan Edwards sometimes scared his weaker sinners into suicide.

McGRATH. As far as my congregation goes, it's their indifference that's suicidal. You can't temporize with Evil!

DUQUESNE. But I'm sure there are people like myself who wonder how a minister who calls himself a Christian can spend quite so much of his time preaching hatred and indignation.

MCGRATH. If you were an honest Christian—

DUQUESNE. I don't call myself a Christian at all.

MCGRATH. Well, if you *were* one, you'd feel indignation, too. Didn't Christ Himself say—

DUQUESNE. That he came not to bring peace but a sword. Jesus did have his militant moments; but in general his doctrine was quite distinct from the policy of the more pugnacious Jews who hadn't yet been intimidated by the Romans—that is, so far as it's possible to tell. We really know very little about him.

MCGRATH. I suppose that by this time you're one of those skeptics who claim that He never existed!

DUQUESNE. Not at all. There's no real way of proving it, but I think it's impossible to doubt that there was someone very remarkable there—a religious leader of genius—who inspired the Christian legend.

MCGRATH. Is that what you're teaching them up there at the college?

DUQUESNE. What I give them is strictly factual— so far as one can know the facts. I don't teach them any theology—except as doctrine that people are known to have believed. As for the divinity of Jesus, I let them make up their own minds.

A knock at the door.

McGrath. Yes?

The Servant appears.

McGrath. Is it the man to fix the window?

The Servant. No, Doctor. It's your brother-in-law on the phone.

McGrath. Tell him I'm busy just now.

The Servant. He wants to know if you're coming out to your sister's funeral.

McGrath reaches his hand toward the telephone on the desk, then decides not to pick up the receiver.

McGrath. Tell him no. Tell him I'll call him later.

The Servant leaves.

McGrath (*to Duquesne*). My sister out in Ohio just died. But I've got to stay here and fight it out. And then my drunken brother-in-law. He ruined my sister's life. He started as an ambulance-chasing lawyer, and now he works in a filling station. If I went out there, I wouldn't be able to see him without telling him what I think of him. Of course, I'll have to pay for the funeral—I suppose you think I ought to forgive him.

Duquesne. He's a very bad lot, is he?

McGrath. He's godless and graceless and gutless. She deserved to get somebody better.

Duquesne. You were fond of your sister?

McGrath (*after a moment's hesitation*). I was fond of her up to the time she married that heel.

—I suppose you'd have me pity and comfort him.

DUQUESNE. I've told you I am not myself a Christian. From my point of view, a bad character is just something that has to be accepted. You can perfectly well not want him around, but when things have gone beyond a certain point, there's no use in being angry.

McGRATH. He'll turn up here and ask for a handout as soon as he's got her buried. And I suppose you think I ought to help him. But I gave him handouts enough as long as Edith was living. This is going to be the end.—And then out there they'd have me at a disadvantage. Once they had me away from my base, they could make it look like an accident.

DUQUESNE. What do you mean? Who do you mean?

McGRATH. The people we've been talking about. You see that broken window.

DUQUESNE. What happened?

McGRATH. They threw a rock through it last night when I was sitting here in my study.

DUQUESNE. That doesn't sound like Communists. It must have been some of these kids. Had you been preaching any sermons against youthful delinquents?

McGRATH. Yes: I certainly had. I said that they ought all to be shipped off to Vietnam.

DUQUESNE. I don't blame them, though, if they don't want to be. They don't believe in the government, they don't believe in religion. They don't want to raise a family and live the way what they call the squares live—so they don't want to learn to do anything, and they don't see any point in staying in college. They don't feel they have anything to live for except hopping themselves up with drugs and sex. They're really dying of boredom. So they make themselves a nuisance for kicks.

McGRATH. And fall into the hands of the Communists. The Communists are behind all these demonstrations.

DUQUESNE. What was it you wanted to talk about?

McGRATH. Well, what I wanted to ask you is this. Tell me, Francis—you're a scholar—(*He hesitates a moment*)—which of the words of Christ may be taken as really authentic?

DUQUESNE. Why, from the scholarly point of view, none of them. The Gospels as we have them must have been written long after Jesus's death. We don't know what he actually said or how much his words may have been edited.

McGRATH. We are told in the Gospels again and again, as well as in the Pauline epistles, that Christ would come back to judge the world.

DUQUESNE. It may very well be that he did say that and that he had really come to believe it.

McGRATH. That He would sit at the right hand of God and separate the sheep from the goats.

Duquesne. It was a very bad time for the Jews. They had been subjugated over and over. When Jesus was crucified, his followers, who believed him to be the Messiah, must have had to imagine that he would vindicate their faith by appearing on the Judgment Day.

McGrath (*not paying much attention*). In Matthew, it is said that He may come like a thief, that we can never know when He is coming.

Duquesne (*smiling*). Yes: it says we must be on the watch.

McGrath. "Then two shall be in the field; the one shall be taken, and the other left."

Duquesne. Yes: the faithful and wise servant is taken, and the evil servant is left.

McGrath. The evil servant has sinned in eating and drinking with the drunken.

Duquesne. But *you* may have erred a little on the other count that is mentioned—that of smiting your fellow-servants.

McGrath. What do you mean?

Duquesne. Why, I mean your attitude at present toward the Communists and the Catholic priests.

McGrath. The Communists and the Catholic priests are no fellow-servants of mine!

Duquesne. They believe, according to their lights, every bit as much as you do that they're serving the best interests of humanity.

McGrath. Your indifference, your infidelity have blunted your moral sense. I don't see how they can trust those young men to such demoralizing tutelage as yours!

DUQUESNE. Well, a good many people would agree with you. That's why I'm out here at this little college instead of in one of the big seminaries. This Protestant Irishman who's President is an out-and-out agnostic who is fully in sympathy with my point of view. He's like something out of the eighteenth century.

MCGRATH. Well, we're in the twentieth now, and we have to fight a form of godlessness that's more terrible than any Voltaireanism.

DUQUESNE. Take it easy, Charley: we're all of us fallible human beings, and we have to get along with one another—even with the Communists and the Catholic priests.

MCGRATH. I am a Christian; you're not.

DUQUESNE. I could never see Calvinism as Christianity. What you *are* is an old-fashioned Calvinist.

MCGRATH. My mother's family in Scotland were Covenanters—in fact, they were straight Cameronians.

DUQUESNE. And fought the Church of England for all they were worth, and hated the other Presbyterians who accepted the authority of the government. Well, I come from the Calvinist tradition, too; but I developed in the other direction. You remember Admiral Duquesne who played such a role under Louis XIV? He refused to forswear his Calvinist faith when the king offered to make him a marshal, but only on condition that he would repudiate Calvinism. That was my father's family, and that's why I went to the Seminary, but I found that I didn't believe and I didn't take orders afterwards. In your case, you've never departed from the original Calvinist bigo- (*Stopping himself from saying "bigotry"*), from the inevitable Calvinist intolerance, which had of course its historical justification. In the early days, Protestantism was wildly centrifugal, and it had to be consolidated. That was the mission of Calvin. He organized the Protestants all over Europe, and he did his best to suppress all those who didn't go along with him. Geneva was the Protestant Kremlin.

McGrath. How can you make such an outrageous statement?!

Duquesne. The Protestants had complained that the Catholic Church didn't want people to read the Bible, because they feared that its inconsistencies would make them ask embarrassing questions; but Calvin, in his *Institutes*, completely refashioned the Bible and provided the Protestants with a new sacred text which seemed to be more consistent because everything human had been excluded. The Jesus Christ of Calvin was no longer a loving Savior; and Calvin had some difficulty in fitting him in to his new theological machine. Since the gulf between God and man is so great, according to Calvin, that, by man's own efforts, he will never

be able to bridge it, God has found it necessary
to send down to earth a part-human divine emissary
to make it possible for man to attain to him. Though
one wonders why God should have gone to this
trouble when the whole situation had been rigged
in advance long before God sent down Jesus. God
had made his arrangements already about who was
to be saved and who was to be damned—and we
must never ask the reasons for his choices. So the
Christian idea that salvation can be granted to anyone who earns it by repenting and accepting Jesus
Christ had, for Calvinism, completely disappeared.

MCGRATH. You could always talk brilliantly,
Francis, but—

DUQUESNE. Please pardon this lecture, Charley.
This habit of expository conversation is an occu-
pational disease, I suppose.

MCGRATH. You're more of a scholar than I am,
but where does all this scholarship get us? I'm not
a theologian—I'm a man of action, and *action* is
what we must have.

DUQUESNE. But do you understand the principles
you act on?—if you'll forgive my going on in this
way. At the Seminary, they softpedaled Calvin.
What we read was old Fuzzy Martin's rather
watered-down version of the *Institutes*. But I
looked the original up, and that's when I ceased
to believe. As Protestants, when we lived in
France, we had had to brace and stiffen ourselves to
hold our own in a Catholic world; but when I

came to grow up in America, there was no such
pressure to pit oneself against, and I found myself
following the development that had led from
Luther to the Enlightenment. *J'ai brulé les
étapes,* as we say—I soon became as centrifugal
as any early non-Calvinist Protestant. What I'm
trying to explain is that you and I are exactly at
opposite poles in representing the different tenden-
cies of Protestantism. You want to lay down the
law—I want to reject authority.

McGrath. (*who has been listening to this with
nervous impatience*). You want to talk about the
past when our whole civilization is menaced.
You're sitting up there at the college playing intellectual games with your students while I'm fighting the battle here alone. Not only do they break
my windows but they write me anonymous letters
and make abusive telephone calls. I suspect that this
room is bugged. I'm going to have the walls exam-
ined when the man comes to fix the window. I
know the house is being watched. Did you notice
that new boy who works for me?

Duquesne. Not particularly. Why?

A knock.

McGrath. Come in.

The Servant. When do you want lunch, Doctor? It's almost one.

McGrath (*to Duquesne*). Will you join me for
lunch?

Duquesne (*rising*). No: I'm sorry—I can't. I'm

lunching with the head of our sociology department to talk about coördinating our courses.

McGrath (*to the Servant*). You can bring my
tray in here. I'll call you in a few minutes.

The Servant goes.

McGrath. I'm sorry you can't stay. I wanted
you to observe him. Would you say he has a good
face or a bad face?

Duquesne. With these beatnik beards they're
wearing, it's hard to tell.

McGrath. I don't like the piercing way he looks
at me—as if he suspected me of something.

Duquesne. He's probably a sharp young Jew.
They're likely to look at you like that. They watch
me in my classes like hawks to see whether they can
catch me out.

McGrath. I don't trust him.

Duquesne. Where did you get him?

McGrath. He answered an ad of mine. I'd had
to let Katy, my Irish girl, go. It's made things very
hard for me lately, because she typed as well as
cooked—but she got to be completely impossible. I
advertized for a secretary who could get me meals,
and this young fellow turned up.

Duquesne. Where does he come from?

McGrath. I haven't been able to find out. He's
very noncommittal about himself. (*Lowering his
voice*) I suspect very strongly he's a Communist.
A good many of the Communists are Jews.

Duquesne. Have you talked to him? You can

usually tell them by the line they take about things.

MᴄGʀᴀᴛʜ. I've never talked to a Communist. (*Suspiciously*) You've evidently seen something of them?

Dᴜǫᴜᴇsɴᴇ. When I worked at a settlement house, just after I got out of the Seminary, I used to make a point of seeing them. I even went to their meetings.—Look, Charley: I think you're up-set by this Allensburg disappointment and the death of your sister—and then this broken window. It's enough to get anybody down.

MᴄGʀᴀᴛʜ. I'm all right, and I'm ready for any-thing. (*He takes a revolver out of a drawer.*) I always keep this on hand.

Dᴜǫᴜᴇsɴᴇ (*laughing*). Well, don't shoot your servant! They're so hard to get nowadays.

MᴄGʀᴀᴛʜ. I'm sure they're out to kill me.

Dᴜǫᴜᴇsɴᴇ. If I were you, I'd see a doctor and tell him about everything that's happened. If he'd send you to a sanitarium, you'd be able to get a rest and you'd be perfectly safe from your enemies.

MᴄGʀᴀᴛʜ. And give up the struggle against Evil? Nay, the gates of Hell shall not prevail against me!

Dᴜǫᴜᴇsɴᴇ. I'll have to go along now. Could I come back for awhile after lunch?

MᴄGʀᴀᴛʜ. You're a scoffer.

Dᴜǫᴜᴇsɴᴇ. I'll promise not to scoff. I'd like to hear more about what you're doing. This reminds me of the old bull sessions that we used to have at the Seminary. So farewell for the present.

He goes out, leaving the door open.

McGRATH (*going to the door, calls*). All right, Jonathan.

Voices of BOYS, *outside the window.* What's happened to Katy Nolan? Where's Katy Nolan?

McGRATH (*going to the window, still with the gun in his hand*). Get out of here! I've got a gun!

Laughter and cries from outside.

McGrath returns to the desk and, still with the revolver in his hand, sits for a moment in thought; then puts the revolver down, picks up the phone and dials a number.

McGRATH (*in answer to the operator*). This is 567-2204.

A moment's wait. He picks up some papers and covers the revolver with them.

VOICE FROM THE TELEPHONE. Hello.

McGRATH. Hello, Fred—Charley speaking. I'm sorry I can't come out, but I'm up to my neck in engagements, and it's most important for me to be here.

FRED's VOICE. We were hoping you'd conduct the service.

McGRATH. After all, perhaps I'm not the right person. I'm sending along a check to cover expenses.—How is your job coming.

FRED's VOICE. It's gone.

McGRATH. What happened?

FRED'S VOICE. It was a wheel I put on came off. It was all my own fault I know. I hadn't screwed it on hard enough. I just did it with my fingers, and I ought to have used a wrench. I was in such a state of mind about Edie!

McGRATH. Was anybody injured?!

FRED'S VOICE. Just a few contusions. Nothing that won't be all right in a couple of months. But they're going to sue the garage, and Joe says that if they get a verdict, he's going to make me pay. But, as a lawyer, I know he can't do it. Actually I'm glad to be rid of that job. I never could get along with Joe: he was always trying to ride me.

McGRATH (*who has been fooling with a paper-knife and otherwise showing signs of impatience*). Well, what are you going to do now?

FRED'S VOICE. I don't know. I've talked to Ed Ferriss about getting a job in the post office, but—

McGRATH. Now, I tell you: you have the funeral parlor send the bill to me, and I'll let you have something to tide you over.

FRED'S VOICE. That's very kind of you, Charley. I—

McGRATH. All right. I'll have to hang up. There's somebody waiting to see me. Sorry I can't get out there. Goodby.

He hangs up and stares angrily at the desk.

JONATHAN *comes in with the lunch tray.*

McGRATH. Put it here on the desk. (*He clears a place, pushing the gun away under the papers.*)

JONATHAN. That soup may taste a little funny. I don't know much about cooking, and I've been studying a recipe book. I tried to make a soup that has curry in it.

MCGRATH. I've told you that I like *plain* food.

JONATHAN. Taste it and see if it's all right.

MCGRATH (*looks down at the soup but does not taste it*). Tell me something about yourself. You're Jewish, aren't you?

JONATHAN. Yes, Doctor.

MCGRATH. An Orthodox Jew?

JONATHAN. No, Doctor.

MCGRATH. Because I don't want to order ham or pork if you're not going to be able to eat it.

JONATHAN. I don't take the Mosaic prohibition as strictly binding any more, but it's hard to break a negative habit. Don't deny yourself on my account, though. I can always eat bread and vegetables.

MCGRATH. You don't belong to a Reformed congregation?

JONATHAN. No, Doctor.

MCGRATH. You're not by any chance a Christian convert?

JONATHAN. Not exactly: no.

MCGRATH. But you do have some knowledge of Christian ideals.

JONATHAN. I've given the subject study.

MCGRATH. My friend who was here just now was telling me my sermons were un-Christian because I'm preaching war on the Communists. Does that seem to you un-Christian?

JONATHAN. Well, the early Christians were Communists.

MCGRATH. That was a quite a different thing. It was the holding of goods in common that one finds in a monastic order. The Communism of our time is an infamous plot to deprive people of their property and turn them against religion. What can we do except exterminate them like vermin?

JONATHAN. Did your friend think we ought to love our enemies the way that Jesus says?

MCGRATH. Christ follows that up by saying, "Do good to them that hate you." Aren't we doing the Communists good by preventing them from doing harm?

JONATHAN. Would you say it was doing people good to drop bombs on them and burn them alive?

MCGRATH. When it's a question of stopping something evil, the more effective the weapons, the better.

JONATHAN. Have you heard about the non-violent resistance movement?

MCGRATH. Rubbish! What would non-violence mean in a practical crisis such as ours in Vietnam? Abandoning the bulwarks we've built against the tide that's been mounting to flood the world!

JONATHAN. Even under Communist domination, the Christian could always say, "Render to Caesar the things that are Caesar's and to God the things that are God's."

McGRATH. You seem to know the Scriptures pretty well for a Jew.—Have you ever had Communist affiliations?

JONATHAN. I was too young in the thirties to go through the Communist phase.

McGRATH. You've taken part in these demonstrations?

JONATHAN. Yes: a couple of times.

McGRATH. That's all the work of the Communists.

JONATHAN. Not these nowadays. Of course, they always try to infiltrate themselves into any movement of protest, but at present they don't count for much. They're not strong enough to capture any movement. I don't think we've got anything to fear like Eastern Europe or Russia.

McGRATH. Were you born in Russia?

JONATHAN. No: I was born in Bethlehem. (*Mc-Grath looks up, startled; then down at the desk, embarrassed.*) Bethlehem, Pennsylvania. But we left there when I was very young.

McGRATH. Where did you grow up?

JONATHAN. In Brooklyn, where my father had a small furniture factory.

McGRATH (*still looking down*). Did you have the usual Jewish education?

JONATHAN. Yes: I went to the yeshiva, if that's what you mean. I was a prize *yeshiva bokher*. (*He smiles.*) I used to dispute with the rabbi. I even wanted to be a rabbi myself.

MᴄGʀᴀᴛʜ (*looking up*). What stopped you?

Jᴏɴᴀᴛʜᴀɴ. I had the curiosity to read up on the literature of Jesus, and I came to the conclusion that Jesus was the greatest of the Jewish prophets —the fullest expression of the will of our God. The later prophets had been leading up to him, and Hillel, the great rabbi, had prepared the way. They were finding that our God was a God of love.

MᴄGʀᴀᴛʜ. And that makes me a bad Christian if my God says, "Vengeance is mine"?

Jᴏɴᴀᴛʜᴀɴ (*with a Jewish gesture of outflung hands*). I am your judge?

McGrath drops his eyes and for a moment is silent.

MᴄGʀᴀᴛʜ. You act as if you were.

Jᴏɴᴀᴛʜᴀɴ. Excuse me. There's the telephone.

He goes out.

McGrath takes up a spoonful of soup, then puts it down again.

MᴄGʀᴀᴛʜ (*muttering to himself*). He said it might taste rather queer. I have to be careful nowadays.

Jonathan reappears.

Jᴏɴᴀᴛʜᴀɴ. It's Deacon Fairchild. He says it's urgent.

McGrath picks up the phone; Jonathan goes.

MᴄGʀᴀᴛʜ. Yes, Deacon.

Voice of Fairchild. There's been vandalism in the church.

McGrath. What? What did they do?

Voice of Fairchild. They broke into the church and did quite a lot of damage. They threw the chairs down from the choir-loft and daubed the pulpit with dirty words in green paint, and they've torn your gown to pieces.

McGrath. The Devil is loose among us! I'll come over as soon as I can. You notify the police.

He puts the receiver down, sit terrifiedly staring a moment, then gets up and goes to the door.

McGrath (*calling*). Jonathan!

Jonathan appears.

McGrath. Did you take those new hymnals to the church?

Jonathan. Yes, Doctor. Last night.

McGrath. Did you notice anything wrong?

Jonathan. No, Doctor. I put them in the racks and piled the old ones up in the vestry.

McGrath. The church has been vandalized.

Jonathan. It must be that River Street gang. They've evidently got it in for you, Doctor.

McGrath. Did you get that green paint for the door?

Jonathan. Yes: I painted part of it this afternoon, and I'll finish it in the morning.

McGrath. Is the pail in the house?

Jonathan. Yes.

McGrath. It's the work of the Devil, like every-thing else!

Jonathan. A possible explanation, Doctor, is that Katy Nolan, who worked for you before, has a young brother who lives down there, and he seems to have a grudge against you.

McGrath. A possible explanation is that you've come to make trouble for me! What are you, I'd like to know. Who are you?

Jonathan. I told you just now, Doctor.

McGrath. You've told me that you were born in Bethlehem and that your father was a carpenter and that, as a boy, you disputed with the rabbis. You want me to think that you're Jesus Christ, and that you've come to reproach me, to judge me. Actually, you're a Communist agent!

Jonathan. I've told you I'm not a Communist.

McGrath. And you told me the Apostles were Communists.

Jonathan. I'm simply here as your servant.

McGrath. The suffering Servant, eh?

Jonathan (*with a Jewish gesture*). I will be if you talk like that, Doctor.

McGrath. You're trying to frighten me with your false divinity, your mouthing of texts, your pretended humility! But I'm able to defend my-self! (*He picks up the revolver from the desk and threatens Jonathan with it.*) Confess that you've come here to terrorize me, to hound me out of my pulpit. A devil in the guise of our Savior! You've been spying on me and you're trying to blackmail me—getting scandal from Katy's brother. You want to give me a bad conscience. Well, the moment has come to end this! Any jury in the world would acquit me!

Jonathan moves backwards to the blank left wall and stretches out his arms in the pose of the Crucified, closing his eyes and dropping his head.

McGrath stands staring and speechless. A long moment of silence; then he drops the hand with the gun.

McGrath (*in a frightened voice*). Is it really Thou—Savior?

Jonathan lifts his head and looks upon McGrath with great compassion and sadness.

McGrath. Hast thou really come again! How base and unworthy I am to have stood in Thy divine presence and not to have recognized Thee! (*He puts down the revolver on the desk and comes forward and falls to his knees.*) Thou accusest me. I know I have sinned. (*Jonathan assumes a sterner look.*) Can anyone since Thou camest to redeem us ever have sinned more grievously than I? God gave me authority, eloquence, a magnetic personality—strength and courage to fight against Evil. I had everything, I thought, in my pride, to make me a great preacher and a consecrated servant of God. But God, who had seen my sin, has known well, in His infinite wisdom, that I should never be able to expiate it and has con-

demned me to remain forever in this unawakened
second-rate town. I have been punished by being
made to preach to these petty and darkened souls
who do not merely not heed me, they hate me. I
am punished, Master, for that which Thou knowest, since I doubt not Thou knowest all things
—for the sins of the flesh, for impurity—for the
impurity of incestuous relations, which is a double
abomination in Thy sight. Hardly can I hope for
forgiveness in pleading that we were young people, my sister and I, alone in the country with our
parents on a poor isolated farm; that we had only
one another for companions, that in childhood we
had slept in the same room, that it was natural for
us as children, when it got to be too cold in winter,
to snuggle up together in the same bed; and that
this later led to what Thou knowest. I won a scholarship—for I showed early promise—went East to
the Seminary. I left her pregnant, though she
never let me know it. She married a good-for-
nothing, and the child was lost. When I went home
and found what had happened, I never wanted to
see her again. I thought about her sometimes with
anguish—driving miles to a beauty parlor to try to
make herself attractive for the miserable wretch
she had married; but I labored and prayed and
wrestled to turn myself into a force for good. Was
all my labor wasted? Can I hope for no pity and
forgiveness? I confess I have sometimes doubted
the strict doctrine of Calvin's *Institutes:* that God

has condemned us from birth. Thou didst come into the world to redeem us, and I have tried to earn my redemption. I have struggled all my life with the flesh, and I have been on the whole successful—though, I own it with remorse, some lapses. This poor girl Katy who worked for me—the Tempter led me astray.

Duquesne has appeared at the door and stands listening.

McGRATH. I could not marry such a girl—and she, of course, a Catholic—it would have hurt my prestige as a preacher—I could hardly have taken her to Allensburg—and I had to send her away to protect myself and her from my passion. Though I gave her a high recommendation in the hope that she would find work elsewhere, I fear her reputation has suffered, and I have earned the bitter indignities to which I am now subjected. Oh, Savior, take pity upon my contrition. She sinned and yet she was innocent. I sinned in seducing her, and now I have sinned in refusing to go to her funeral!

Duquesne comes forward from the doorway; McGrath looks around blankly. Duquesne puts his hand on his shoulder.

DUQUESNE. Look, Charley: I'm sorry to intrude on your devotions, but I think that I ought to tell you that you're laboring under a misapprehension. This boy is not Jesus Christ: he's a sociology major from the college. I've just had lunch with our sociology man, and he told me all about him. He took this job with you here as an assignment in sociological field work.

McGrath looks up at him dazed. Jonathan has dropped his arms.

McGrath. The sociologists are part of the conspiracy!

Duquesne. You'd better get up, old man. I've brought the doctor from the college, and I think that you ought to see him.

McGrath (*rising to his feet*). What can a doctor do for me?

Duquesne. He can give you a tranquillizer and perhaps relieve your mind.

McGrath. How do I know that he isn't one of them?

Duquesne. We screen our doctors very carefully. I assure you that there's no conspiracy.

He takes McGrath's arm and leads him out.

Jonathan flexes his arms, then picks up the revolver and puts it in his pocket.

Duquesne comes back into the room.

Jonathan. That was a tough one.

Duquesne. I could see.

Jonathan. I'm sorry I had to hear his confession, but he was on the point of shooting me.—Here, you better take this gun. (*He hands Duquesne the revolver.*) He imagined I was a Communist pretending to be Jesus, so I thought I could only save my life by pretending that I *was* Jesus. The whole thing was very embarrassing, and it's hard to keep in that position—as if you were nailed up.

DUQUESNE. As a student of sociology, what conclusions did you come to about the Doctor?

JONATHAN. I don't think he's difficult to analyze. From the psychological point of view, he's got a long-standing neurosis—a tie-up with this sister who just died. Now he always has to repudiate his women the way he did her. That's what happened with this maid he just dismissed. From the economic standpoint, he's terrified that the Communists will take over the country and that he won't have any more job. I tried to reassure him about that, but he's too paranoiac now to be reassured. In the sociological connection, he can't get more than six or seven thousand a year, and that creates a servant problem. He wants somebody to do everything for him here—cooking and housework and secretarial work for fifty dollars a week. And he made this girl Katy go to bed with him.

But I really feel sorry for him. He's had to spend his whole life pretending. A Jew may have to do a certain amount of pretending, but usually not on that scale. It's been hard enough for me this week to pretend to be a butler—and to have to pretend to be Jesus!

McGrath comes back from the other room.

DUQUESNE. Did he give you a tranquillizer?

MCGRATH. Yes.—I want to do some private phoning.

DUQUESNE. All right: we'll leave you alone.—
Are you sure that you're quite all right?

McGRATH. Yes: I'm going to do what you think
Jesus wants me to.

JONATHAN. Let me know if you want anything,
Doctor.

They go out.

McGrath dials and gives his number.

*A Carpenter appears at the door. He has a strange
swarthy face, beardless but with heavy eye-brows.*

THE CARPENTER. Is it all right to work on the
window?

McGrath looks up startled and stares at him.

McGRATH. Go ahead. You won't disturb me.
(*To the telephone, with difficulty controlling his
voice.*) Hello, Fred, I've decided to come out, after
all, but I can't perform the service. This whole
thing has very much—broken me up. Yes: I'm getting a reservation for tomorrow morning. You
don't need to meet me.

He hangs up.

McGRATH (*to the carpenter, who has been taking out the broken panes and measuring the window frame*). I was afraid you weren't coming today. It's important to get it repaired.

THE CARPENTER. Have you got the wooden
frame?

*McGrath gets it out of the wastebasket. The
Carpenter holds it up, and it is seen to be cruci-
form, but broken.*

McGrath. Can't you finish it up tonight?

The Carpenter. I'll have to make a new frame, and that'll take a little time.

McGrath. Well, please get it done as soon as you can.

The Carpenter. I'll try to do it sometime to-morrow.

McGrath. All right. Please see that you do.

The Carpenter picks up his kit and goes out.

McGrath picks up the Bible and opens it, as if he were looking for a text; then puts it down and sinks on the desk, his hands clasping his head.

McGrath. Oh, Edie, I thought you'd be so proud of me!

The Voice of the Carpenter (*speaking clearly from nowhere*). And my work was accomplished here by an atheist and a Jew.

McGrath takes down his hands and looks up.

OSBERT'S CAREER, OR
THE POET'S PROGRESS

1926-1968

Osbert was begun in the middle twenties, added to at the beginning of the thirties and finished in 1968. I seem, in the first three acts, to have made some fairly accurate predictions.

The satire on the "Humanism" of Irving Babbit and Paul Elmer More, which had at the time a certain academic vogue, will hardly be understood by members of a later generation, and such satire is today hardly needed.

ACT I

SCENE 1

Mrs. Rosemary's sitting-room. It is decorated in lavender, pink and white: there are large pink roses on the wall-paper and, on a little table in the right-hand corner (from the actor's point of view), with pink bows tied around their necks, roses of impossible size in a vase. A pink sofa on the left; a door leading to the street at the left of the back wall and another door on the right, leading into the house; a window, with lavender curtains, in the back at the right. A desk, with a calendar and a clock, against the left wall behind the couch. There is a waste-basket with a pink bow beside it.

Mrs. Rosemary, dressed in lavender in a style suggesting the end of the last century—high collar with pink bow, corseted waist and long full skirts—comes in through the door on the right, crosses over to the opposite side of the room and tears the number 31 off the calendar—she smartly crumples it into a ball and drops it into the waste-paper basket; then briskly glances at the clock. Though costumed like a kind of bonbon, she is decisive and very firm.

Mrs. Rosemary. It's nearly half past nine: I must get him off.—Osbert!

Osbert (*appearing from the right-hand door*). Yes, Mother dear.

He is dressed in a deeper shade of purple, with belling sailor's trousers and an enormous Eton collar with a silk bow-tie of deep rose-color. His hair is parted in the middle.

Mrs. Rosemary. It's almost time for you to go: are you ready? This is the day for you to leave, you know.

Osbert. I'm not quite packed yet, Mother dear.

Mrs. Rosemary. Good heavens! What have you been doing?

Osbert. It was so lovely I went for a walk.

Mrs. Rosemary. My dear, when you begin to work, you'll have to learn to be more punctual. I really don't know how you're going to get on. But I couldn't think of anything better for you to do. You're not active enough for the Army and you haven't enough money for politics. You're not interested in Medicine or Law. And the Church has gone completely bankrupt.

Osbert. Yes, Mother dear: I know.

Mrs. Rosemary. The only thing you can do is write poetry, and poetry is not a profession. But your work in the paperweight factory won't prevent you from writing, too. They're very old friends of ours and belong to the old pre-industrial world of distinguished handicraft.

Osbert. Yes, Mother: I've come to believe that the only hope for modern civilization is simply in making beautiful things. I feel that a real poet designing really beautiful paperweights might help to transform the world.

Mrs. Rosemary. Well, my dear, you must be content at first to learn your trade very patiently and humbly. (*She sits down on the sofa, and Osbert sits down beside her.*) Though you won't have to do any real drudgery: the Megrims' business isn't like a modern factory. The Megrims aren't really business people at all—they were formerly attached to the Court.

Osbert. Yes, of course, Mother dear: I know.

Mrs. Rosemary. With the exception of ourselves, in fact, the Megrims are almost the only family left who still lives in their original stone house. They and we and a very few others. That is a very great distinction and one that you should be very proud of. When you get to Mr. Rudolf's Town tomorrow, you will find all the houses made of glass—and the people who live in glass houses aren't the same as the old race.

Osbert. Yes, Mother dear—of course. I know what it means to be a stone-house man.

Mrs. Rosemary. But you have never seen the glass-house civilization. In the places where everything is made of glass, the roofs of people's houses are always cracking and their floors breaking up under their feet. They never feel themselves really safe, so they can never accomplish anything really sound. Why, if they even try to stain their own glass, their houses are taken away by Mr. Rudolf and melted up in the common foundry!

OSBERT. Yes, Mother: I think it's disgusting.

MRS. ROSEMARY. So you must remember always, my dear, no matter how far away from home you may be, that your standards are stone-house standards—that you do not belong to the world of glass. You must remember that there are certain things which a stone-house man is obliged to do, no matter whether the glass-house people do them or not, and that there are things which you mustn't do, even though everybody else does them. The principles of the glass-house people are always being shattered to bits or being melted down to cheap easy materials. But the honor of a stone-house man must stand fast and endure like stone!

OSBERT. You know that Dominic the Dolmen has always been my favorite hero, Mother dear!

VOICES OUTSIDE THE WINDOW. Berty! Oh Berty!

MRS. ROSEMARY (*getting up*). There are Queenie and Lucille come to say goodby.

Queenie and Lucille come in from the street: they are pretty little girls with hair-ribbons. Queenie, the younger, in pale pink, is a blonde; Lucille, in red, a brunette.

QUEENIE. We've brought you some goodby presents, Berty!

MRS. ROSEMARY. Oh, how nice!

Osbert. You oughtn't to have done that!

Queenie. Why, we wouldn't let you go without a present to remember us by! It's going to be months before we see you again!—This is a pincushion, Berty—I thought you'd probably need one. (*She presents him with a round pink pincushion.*)

Osbert. Oh, what a lovely color! What a lovely shape! How sweet of you to think of it, Queenie! I'll never stick a pin in my pin-cushion without remembering you!

Lucille (*producing a large pocket-knife*). I thought you might need a knife: I knew you didn't have one.

Osbert. Oh, thank you—thank you, Lucille! I've never been able to keep a knife—I've always lost them right away. But I'll keep this one forever! It's the most beautiful knife I've ever seen! With three blades!—and what's this?

Lucille. That's a thing to punch holes with.

Mrs. Rosemary. An awl.

Osbert. And what's this? A corkscrew! How marvelous!

Mrs. Rosemary (*smiling*). I hope you won't need that too often.

Queenie. Oh, Berty! what shall we ever do without you? You must write to us often and often!

Osbert. I will: and you must write me, too—you and Lucille both.

Queenie. Oh, we will! we will!

Mrs. Rosemary. I must go up and get his shawl-strap packed: the carriage will be here in a minute.

Queenie. Oh, do let me help, Mrs. Rosemary! I love to pack people's things!

Mrs. Rosemary (*to Osbert*). Now don't wander away while I'm gone: you've got to make connections with the coach.

Osbert. All right, Mother dear: I won't.

Mrs. Rosemary and Queenie go out through the door on the right. As soon as they have gone, Osbert swiftly comes over to Lucille and takes her by the hands.

Osbert. I couldn't pack last night: I was thinking all the time of you! When I came back, after we'd been together, things like packing didn't seem real! I didn't even take off my clothes! I didn't even sleep! I couldn't do anything but make up poetry!

He makes her sit down on the sofa, still holding her hands.

Lucille. Foolish: you ought to have got some sleep.

Osbert. Oh, Lucille—the only way I could tell what I feel would be to show you what I wrote, and though I think it's the very best I ever did, it seems stupid to me when I see you!—Let me say it to you now, Lucille!

Lucille. You mustn't miss the coach.

Osbert. This is about when I was waiting in the garden—when I was afraid that you wouldn't come—when I was afraid that if you did come, I

shouldn't dare to kiss you. I couldn't believe then
that I ever should!

LUCILLE. I was scared you wouldn't, too.

OSBERT. This is what I wrote—

Along the garden where you came
    I envied wild inhuman things—
The dahlias fierce, dilating flame,
    The spiders dizzy in their swings—

LUCILLE (*laughing*). The way Queenie gets,
eh?

OSBERT. But I really saw it all like that!

Gay tulips globing golden shouts—
    Snapdragons bridling, dazed, to bite—
Brown columbine with quivering snouts,
    Like prowling boars surprised by light!

While I—I praying most for power,
    While stalks and stems were thrilled to life,
Stand rooted, dumb and futile as a flower
    Before the drought, the tempest or the knife.

LUCILLE. You oughtn't to be so shy. I guess you
won't be that way long, after you've been in Mr.
Rudolf's Town!

OSBERT. It wasn't shyness: it was you! When I
see you, a shuddering shakes me!

LUCILLE. Father scolded me because the ham-
mock broke.

OSBERT. Oh, I'm so sorry! It was all my fault.

LUCILLE. I don't care!

OSBERT. And I don't care about anything but you and that I'm going away from you!

LUCILLE. Oh, take me with you, Berty!

OSBERT. I can't now.—But I'll have you come on later. I thought about it all last night.

LUCILLE. You may forget about me in Mr. Rudolf's Town, when you get to be a millionaire.

OSBERT. I shan't be a millionaire. I don't care anything about making money. That's the trouble with Mr. Rudolf's civilization—nobody cares about anything but money.—I want to create beautiful things that will make people forget about money. An artist can be a much greater person than a millionaire, Lucille. If a man could bring back Beauty to Mr. Rudolf's civilization, the people would fall down on their knees! Compared to him, Mr. Rudolf would seem like an ugly toad.

LUCILLE. I hope that you'll make enough money to send me my fare to the big Town. I'm tired and sick of it here. Father won't let me have any fun. I want to get away to the Town.

OSBERT. Oh, I shall, I hope—I shall!

Mrs. Rosemary and Queenie come back from upstairs: Mrs. Rosemary has Osbert's shawl-strap, a purple and pink plaid, tied up with a large pink bow.

QUEENIE. I packed your things myself, Berty! I put in some pressed rose-leaves!

OSBERT. Oh, thank you so much, Mother dear.

MRS. ROSEMARY (*who has just been to the window*). The carriage is here: it's time for you to go.

OSBERT (*in a low voice to Lucille*). I'll write a poem about you every day. And you'll come on and we'll be married!

MRS. ROSEMARY (*coming over and helping him on with his plum-colored cloak*). Don't forget to tip the driver, Osbert; and put your muffler on during the night: you mustn't catch cold in the coach. (*She hands him a sort of truncated high hat, also purple.*)

OSBERT. Yes, Mother dear.

QUEENIE. I think we ought to kiss him goodby, now that he's going away for so long!

She kisses him and then Lucille kisses him: he kisses Lucille earnestly back.

LUCILLE (*sotto voce*). See you soon in Mr. Rudolf's Town, maybe?

OSBERT (*to Lucille*). Yes: I'll write—and you must write me often!

QUEENIE. Oh, we will—we will.

MRS. ROSEMARY. Come, my dear: you must go!

She pilots him out the door. The girls stand looking after him.

QUEENIE and LUCILLE (*waving their handkerchiefs*). Goodby! Goodby! (*Then louder, turning toward the right, as the carriage drives off*) Goodby! Goodby! (*Sending their voices further*) Goodby!

LUCILLE (*turning back to the room*). He's turned the corner: he's gone.

QUEENIE (*still waving out the door*). Goodbyee! Goodbyee!

SCENE 2

Old Mrs. Megrim's drawing-room, all in anti-quated browns and yellows. Two doors, at stage right and left, the former leading into the house and the latter to the street door. At the back, a fireplace with a mantel, and on the mantel, a most elaborate clock encrusted with a bristling bronze "allegory" of mythological figures with helmets and spears; above the clock, a family portrait of some semi-royal personage in an elaborate military uniform and wig. On either side of the fireplace, in which a fire is burning, framed water-color designs for paperweights— they are all in the form of glass globes with little figures inside. On the right and further forward than the door, a glass cabinet for old china and precious old paperweights. Three old-fashioned chairs and a sofa, making a semicircle which faces the audience and of which the right-hand arm is the sofa. In the chair at the extreme left, old Mrs. Megrim is sitting: she is very shrunken and bent and dressed in dull brown: she wears a large lace-bordered bonnet with a visor which completely hides her face. Her son Harry, a blurred and gray-faced man of indeterminable age, with eye-glasses askew on his nose and a light brown suit which needs pressing, is introducing Osbert to his mother. They talk loudly to old Mrs. Megrim, because she is very deaf.

OLD MRS. MEGRIM (*very senile, but with a certain social vigor*). Well, Osbert Rosemary—a man! When I last saw you, you were a tiny little boy. To think that Marguerite Rosemary should have a grown-up son! I always remember your mother, Osbert, as she was when I first knew her. She was the prettiest girl I think I ever saw. The year she came out, she was the belle of the season. I remember her so vividly at the antelope races! They used to say that there were more people looking at Marguerite Rosemary than watching the antelopes! And then her marriage was so romantic! When she ran away with your father, she left all her suitors gasping: they hadn't counted on being jilted for a man who came from the forests and whom nobody had ever known. He abandoned her as we feared he would, and she dropped her rather grotesque married name. I am told you more resemble your mother, but my poor old eyes are so weak that I am hardly aware nowadays of what my own son Harry looks like! (*Harry Megrim laughs self-consciously and foolishly.*) I have to be content to know people through the eyes of the spirit merely—and that is perhaps as good a way as any with those who are near and dear to us. (*She very slowly and feebly opens a bag that draws with a cord at the neck, and takes out a mothball, which she puts into her mouth.*) I won't offer you a mothball, Osbert: they are only for old folks like me: I know that a young fellow like you would scarcely consider them a delicacy!

HARRY MEGRIM (*motioning Osbert toward the sofa*). Do—please sit down, won't you? (*He speaks stutteringly and blurtingly.*)

OSBERT. Thank you.

He sits down, but the seat of the sofa collapses, subsiding to the level of the floor.

HARRY MEGRIM. Oh, I'm afraid you're not comfortable like that! Our furniture is so inefficient— I mean to say old-ficient—I mean to say, old-fashioned!

OSBERT. Oh, no; I'm quite comfortable, thank you.

OLD MRS. MEGRIM (*who cannot see what has happened*). That sofa belonged to my great-uncle Jerolemon—your great-great uncle, Harry.

HARRY MEGRIM. Are you sure you're quite comfortable there?

OSBERT. Yes, thank you: perfectly comfortable.

OLD MRS. MEGRIM. We have invited Mr. Trixie and Mr. Tiralira to come in this afternoon. We thought that it would be nice for you to meet them. They are new friends of ours, to be sure, but we have come to prize them highly. Mr. Trixie is such a gifted man—so sensitive and so fervent—and

Mr. Tiralira is a connoisseur of such distinguished taste!

Harry Megrim. And such a delightful fellow!

Old Mrs. Megrim. And such a charming gentleman! Mr. Trixie and Mr. Tiralira have been kind enough—I should even perhaps say, they have been heroic enough—to devote their energies and abilities—which, in these days of great industries and great fortunes, could be so much more profitably employed elsewhere—to what I may call the aesthetic department of our own humble little business—I hardly dare call it an industry! We have felt that new blood was needed—I am sadly behind the times—but Harry follows the fads and the fashions, and the modern taste, it seems, demands novelty and innovation. So Mr. Trixie and Mr. Tiralira have done us the honor of bringing to our problems their experience and mature wisdom, and now we shall have also to inspire us the creative spirit of youth. We expect from you, dear Osbert, new designs even more alluring and astonishing than any which have yet been evolved—with the paperweights, in short, of a poet! I am sorry that I shall not be able to see them, but perhaps, after all, that is just as well, for I am sure that, much as I should admire them, I should not understand them at all! (*She laughs and takes another mothball.*)

Harry Megrim (*indicating the drawings on either side of the fireplace*). Those are both designs by Mr. Trixie. That—that one's the Little Torpedo

—and that—that's the Iron Pansy—the Iron Pansy, you know is Mr. Rudolf's symbol—and that—that one's the Rudolf Monument. Quite up to the moment, you see!

OLD MRS. MEGRIM. I shall never get used to it! Our paperweights used all to be flowers or ferns or mythological figures!

Harry has opened the cabinet and taken out a large antique paperweight. He shows it to Osbert and then shakes it: the liquid inside the glass ball clouds up with little flakes.

HARRY MEGRIM. This is the "Eidelweiss in a Snowstorm."

OSBERT (*getting up to look at it*). How lovely!

HARRY MEGRIM (*bringing out another*). This— this is Danaë and the Golden Shower. It's really an awfully fine one.

OLD MRS. MEGRIM. Yes: the Danaë! Mr. Tiralira considers it the most perfect paperweight ever made.

OSBERT. Oh, what a beautiful one! Let me see it! —How fresh and bright the gold still is!

HARRY MEGRIM (*as the doorbell rings*). I think that must be them now.

He goes out at the left.

OLD MRS. MEGRIM. I have always thought it would have been in better taste for Mr. Rudolf to have left it to posterity to erect a monument in his honor. But he wanted to be sure it did him justice, I suppose!

Harry comes back with Mr. Trixie and Mr. Tiralira. Mr. Trixie wears an artist's yellow tie, a Van Dyck beard, a green velvet jacket and yellow trousers. Mr. Tiralira, who is tall and slender, wears a light pea-green suit, with lavender spats and a pink handkerchief sticking out of his pocket.

MR. TIRALIRA (*effusively and gaily, advancing toward Mrs. Megrim*). And how is the loveliest woman in the world? The wittiest, the wisest, the most gracious! The sovereign of all our hearts! The eternal toast of the season! (*He shakes hands with her so vigorously that her wrist breaks and her hand comes off in his.*) Oh, how dreadful! I'm so dreadfully sorry!

HARRY MEGRIM (*taking the hand from him*). It really doesn't matter. Mother's getting so dilapidated —I mean to say, debilitated!

He carefully puts the hand away in the china cabinet and replaces the paperweights.

OLD MRS. MEGRIM. It will be quite easy to have it mended. I fear that I'm becoming a little brittle— like old porcelain, you know! (*She laughs coquettishly.*)

MR. TIRALIRA (*bowing*). And even more precious!

OLD MRS. MEGRIM. I shouldn't bring a very high price today, I'm afraid: after all, I'm not made of *glass!*—And now I must present Mr. Osbert Rose-

mary—the young man of whom I was telling you
—the son of very dear old friends of ours. This is
Mr. Trixie, Osbert—and Mr. Tiralira. (*The visitors and Osbert shake hands.*) You must forgive me
—I am so blind that I can't see where you are!

MR. TRIXIE. What an enchanting old house, Mrs.
Megrim! What fascinating old things! It always
makes me want to weep to see them—to think that
the art of making lovely things should almost have
perished from the earth!

OLD MRS. MEGRIM. The furniture in this room
was given to my great-grandfather by Prince Louis.
It was made for him by the royal cabinetmaker.

MR. TRIXIE. Ah, say what you like, Mrs. Megrim! There can be no high beauty of living without high distinction of blood. In Prince Louis's
days, a lady's drawing-room was as truly a work
of art as a miniature or a fugue. Today the glass
manufacturers and their government have vul-
garized our whole civilization. Why, I wouldn't
give a single chair in this room for the glass government and all its works! (*Osbert has resumed his
seat on the sunken sofa; Mr. Tiralira is posted by
the arm of Mrs. Megrim's chair; Harry has sat
down in the chair nearest the sofa. Now Mr. Trixie
seats himself between Harry and Mrs. Megrim,
voluptuously stroking the arms of the chair.*) See:
the lines of this lovely thing are like the strains of
a violin!

As he settles himself, the back breaks and he falls over backwards on to the floor. Mr. Tiralira and Harry spring forward to help him up.

OLD MRS. MEGRIM (*who is unaware of what has happened, taking a mothball with her remaining left hand*). I won't offer you a mothball, Mr. Trixie: they are only for old people like me!

HARRY MEGRIM. Oh, dear! I hope you didn't get broken! I mean I hope you didn't get hurt!

MR. TRIXIE (*now on his feet and rubbing the back of his head*). Oh, no! I'm not hurt! Not at all! But I'm perfectly sick about the chair!

HARRY MEGRIM (*flustered and apprehensive*). About the what? Where is it you feel badly?

MR. TRIXIE. I mean, I'm broken-hearted about the chair!

MR. TIRALIRA. What a pity that these exquisite old things should be subjected to every-day use! They should really be preserved in a museum. I was speaking of it to Mr. Rudolf only the other day. Mr. Rudolf, my dear Mrs. Megrim, is a man of really fine taste. We are in the habit of judging him unfairly—of assuming that he is ignorant and vulgar. But though he rose from such humble beginnings, he has a strongly individual sense of beauty. He is a collector—in fact, the chief living authority on German imperial mustache cups and old American cigar-bands; and he has what is probably the most complete collection in the world of stickpins made of stuffed goldfish. One might wish him to collect other things perhaps! but it at least shows an original taste for the curious and the exotic. I was telling him only the other day about your beautiful house, and he said at once that he would like to preserve it—to have it set up just as it is in his museum. He asked whether you would care to sell it, and even named a very generous figure—if any price can be put upon the inestimable!

While he has been talking, Mr. Tiralira has been leaning on the end of the mantelpiece, which is loose and has tipped up at an angle, so that the clock has been sliding down in his direction. Harry Megrim has been watching it anxiously.

HARRY MEGRIM. Look out for that allegory! It's a horrid thing to be spiked by!

MR. TIRALIRA (*taking his arm off, as Harry replaces the clock*). Now in the museum they would have that fastened down; they would make it impossible for such a thing to happen. Think if that wonderful old clock had fallen! What an irreparable loss!

MR. TRIXIE. Can you really believe that those vandals would know how to take care of these treasures?

MR. TIRALIRA. I believe, as I have just been saying, that you quite misconceive Mr. Rudolf. In any case, he is sending an Emissary to discuss the matter with Mrs. Megrim. I hope you will receive him,

dear lady. I think you will find that Mr. Rudolf is
fully sensible of the consideration due you.

*Mr. Rudolf's Emissary suddenly enters from
the door on the right. He is a spare man dressed
in a dark uniform, with a sharp nose and a small
mustache. With a swift glance he picks out Mrs.
Megrim and goes straight over to her. He does
not remove his high black derby.*

THE EMISSARY. Mrs. Westermountain Megrim?

OLD MRS. MEGRIM. I am Mrs. Megrim.

THE EMISSARY (*producing a paper*). I have here
an agreement for transference of property drawn
up in the government offices and signed by Mr.
Rudolf. According to this agreement, your house
and the contents of the house are to be taken over
by Mr. Rudolf's government for the sum of thirty
thousand zukors.

OLD MRS. MEGRIM. Indeed? That is very generous. But I am afraid it is out of the question.

THE EMISSARY. I must advise you that, should
you fail to accept these terms, the house and its
contents will be confiscated on an order of the
Ministry of Monuments.

OLD MRS. MEGRIM. What is it he says, Harry?

MR. TIRALIRA (*intervening*). Only think what it
would mean to you, dear lady! Thirty thousand
zukors! You would be free to travel and to live as
you pleased! You could go to the Spa every summer—you could resume your old social sovereignty!

HARRY MEGRIM. It—it sounds like a square meal —I mean to say a square deal!

THE EMISSARY. It has been brought to Mr. Rudolf's attention that H. P. Megrim & Son have been operating a small glass plant independent of the Government Glass Works. This plant has been used for the manufacture of paperweights of a kind not approved by the government and no longer in demand. I must advise you that all materials and tools employed in unauthorized glass-manufacture are to be surrendered to the Central Glass Works within ten days after the order has been issued. In compensation for these tools and materials, which are obsolete and of little value, you will receive an additional five thousand zukors.

MR. TIRALIRA (*to Harry*). But consider, dear old boy! Thirty-five thousand zukors! Why, you could begin breeding owls again! It would give you a new lease on life! You know that you would rather breed owls than do anything else in the world! Don't deny it, old boy! It's your vocation and your gift! And Mr. Rudolf has told me confidentially that he will offer you a post in his aviary.

OLD MRS. MEGRIM. It is kind of Mr. Rudolf, Harry, to wish to make it possible for you to breed owls again!

MR. TRIXIE. But what about us, Archy? We can't work for the Central Glass Works!

MR. TIRALIRA. But why can't we, my dear boy? Mr. Rudolf will offer us places. He is most eager to have you take over the portfolio of Officers' Uniforms.

MR. TRIXIE. Oh, dear: I'm so easily influenced! I'm afraid I shall allow myself to be persuaded! And what sort of a job will *you* get?

MR. TIRALIRA. Mr. Rudolf has been flattering enough to offer me the curatorship of his museum. And you, my dear boy (*turning to Osbert*): you love literature—you are a poet. You will operate the electric ladders in Mr. Rudolf's library. You will love it! You will be mad about it! Mr. Rudolf is a book collector, and his library contains nothing but first editions. You will get a thousand zukors a year.

OSBERT (*spiritedly and proudly*). I will never work in Mr. Rudolf's library! I will never work for Mr. Rudolf at all! My people are stone-house people, and my standards are stone-house standards! What do I care about Mr. Rudolf's money and his library and his museum? The work I do, I do for its own sake—the things I make, I make for their own sake! Not to live in a ridiculous palace and try to buy what I can't create. And the things that I make will be all new-born—not old first editions in a library. They will be forces that you cannot control!

The Emissary blows a police whistle and two uniformed guards march in from the left-hand door. The Emissary indicates Osbert with a single

*sharp gesture of the thumb; and the guards snap
handcuffs on him.*

THE EMISSARY. You will proceed at once to the
Desert, where you will be taught the duties of a
sand shoveller.

MR. TIRALIRA (*shaking one of Osbert's manacled
hands and clapping him on the shoulder*). Go in
and win, old boy! It's an arduous exacting life; but
there are big rewards for a lad of pluck!

OSBERT (*scornfully*). Rewards! What do I care
for their silly rewards?

*One of the guards claps a hand over his mouth
and seizes him under the arms, and the other
takes him by the feet: they swiftly carry him out.*

OLD MRS. MEGRIM. That was bravely spoken,
Osbert! How I wish I could see you standing
there, in all the pride and candor of youth, defying
the forces that bid fair to undo us! We cannot have
you to work with us now—I am sorry, but I know
that it will be no hardship not to be wasting the
years of your youngmanhood in our poky old-
fashioned business. I am old and I must surrender.
But you have youth and courage and strength. Go
forth like a clear-eyed knight, Osbert! Fight the
fight of a stone-house man—and maintain stone-
house honor uncracked!

THE EMISSARY (*to Mr. Tiralira*). Make them
sign: I must go. (*He hands the agreement to
Harry.*)

HARRY MEGRIM (*looking at the paper bewilder-*

edly). But I don't understand it very well! Suppose we should sign everything away and then find ourselves completely prostitute—I mean to say, destitute!

THE EMISSARY. Where is the ink?

MR. TIRALIRA. In the library.—(*To Harry*) Come along, old boy!

Mr. Tiralira and the Emissary, taking Harry by either arm—Mr. Tiralira on Harry's right and the Emissary on the side toward the audience— steer him out through the door at the right.

THE EMISSARY (*to Mr. Tiralira*). Make an inventory at once and mail it to me tonight.

MR. TIRALIRA (*clapping the Emissary on the shoulder*). Right you are! Good-night, old boy!

He goes out with Harry. The Emissary, as they leave him at the door, finds that Harry Megrim's arm has come off in his hand. He regards it without emotion.

OLD MRS. MEGRIM. Yet it was truly kind of Mr. Rudolf to wish me to go to the Spa!

MR. TRIXIE. Yes: we shouldn't remember it against him that he was once only a button peddler. His energy and character are magnificent! They have the beauty of some sinewy bronze!

The Emissary goes over to the fireplace and sticks Harry's arm in the grate: he shoves it into the fire with his foot, then quickly goes out at the left.

OLD MRS. MEGRIM. How brightly the fire burns!

I can see it quite plainly now! It reminds me of the autumn days when I first knew your father, Harry —we used to come back from the antelope races and sit around the fire here—we used to talk and drink peach-punch and play forfeits—sometimes the forfeit was a kiss. It brings all our courtship back!

ACT II

SCENE 1

The Great Desert: a sand-sifting station. On the right is a high wall cutting across the back corner of the stage and showing dark against the blue western light of the late afternoon: a guard with a rifle on his shoulder is seen to pace along the top from time to time. Below the wall is a sand-sifters' one-room shack, one side of which is open to the audience and which occupies most of the stage. The shack is made of glass, but opaque: a doorway on the right, and small windows, two in the back and one in the right-hand wall between the back and the door. At the left, a plain deal table with a red cotton cloth, some cutlery and plates, cups, pitchers, etc. in thick white ware: two chairs are drawn up beside it. There is a clothes-line, with shirts and underclothes on it, stretched between the shack and the wall on the farther side of the door. Two army cots at the back.

At the left of the shack, Osbert Rosemary and another older man are working mechanical sandsifters. These are sieves which are shaken back and forth by turning a crank: they are fed from a *large reservoir on the roof, from which the sand runs down into the sieves through a double funnel mouth; below the sieves are larger cylindrical jars, into which the sifted sand falls. The two men stand sifting in silence, Osbert facing the audience and his companion further forward and in profile. Both are dressed in blue sand-sifters' overalls and coarse shirts open at the neck. The older man is bald and wears spectacles and a black skull-cap.*

Osbert at last speaks.

OSBERT. It must be nearly five.

DR. DISH. I don't think so: it was only half past three when I last looked. (*A silence*) The days are getting shorter: it gets dark earlier now.

OSBERT. Do we have tooth-mug inspection to-morrow?

DR. DISH. Yes.

Silence.

DR. DISH. Did I ever tell you how we ragged Professor Groper when I was a student at the old University?

OSBERT. I don't remember.

DR. DISH. Old Groper had a horse-hair wig—people wore them in those days—at least people without taste did—and old Groper was certainly no dandy. I was just about to graduate—but old Groper would not let me take honors. I was im-measurably his most brilliant pupil—I think I may

say it now without vanity—but I had refuted all his
conclusions about the First Dolichocephalic War. I
had even had the temerity—or perhaps I should say
I had had the impudence—to make it the subject of
my thesis, and old Groper never forgave me.

   *Osbert looks about him, drops the sifter and
   throws a small rolled document over the wall.*

OSBERT. There goes another poem.

DR. DISH. You'll get in trouble doing that some
day.

OSBERT. This one's not subversive—just melan-
choly.

DR. DISH. Well, old Groper, as I was saying,
revenged himself by withholding my honors. The
time came for graduation, and old Groper had to
preside. My chums and I put our heads together—
I had many friends in those days—and we hit upon
a plan. We went out and caught some biri-biri birds
which were nesting in an old livery stable. Biri-biri
birds build their nests with horse-hair, you know.
Well, on the day of graduation, old Groper turned
up with his horse-hair wig in more than usually
slovenly condition. We had put the biri-biri birds in
boxes—

OSBERT. Oh, yes: I remember now: you *have* told
me that story.

DR. DISH. Yes: I suppose I have.

   *Another silence: they go on sifting. Two fig-
   ures come in at the right outside the shack: one
   is a guard, the other a tall man in his middle for-*

*ties, with a gaudy plaid suit, a green derby and a
very large polka-dotted bow tie: he has red hair
and a red bloated face, and his mustache and his
hair along his forehead are arranged in rakish
curls.*

BIMBO. What is this, for God's sake?—a jail?

THE GUARD. No, buddy: not a jail—an industrial
training camp.

BIMBO. Industrial training camp be damned! I
was brought here against my will!

THE GUARD. You'll find you like it here, buddy.
Everybody settles down.

*Just as they reach the door of the shack, Bimbo
turns and looks up the wall.*

BIMBO. What a splendid wall! How high is it?

THE GUARD. Eighty bisters, buddy.

*Bimbo pretends to admire the wall, while the
Guard is opening the door, but suddenly snatches
for the Guard's pistol, which the latter carries in
a holster on his hip. There is a short violent struggle of which Bimbo gets the worse. The Guard
shoves him off and leaves.*

THE GUARD (*shouting in at the door, before
slamming it to*). Try that again, buddy, and you'll
get sand-papered!

BIMBO (*opening the door and shouting out*). Try
that sand-paper on your ass, buddy! (*Turning to
Osbert and Dr. Dish, and taking off his hat*) I hope
you will forgive me, gentlemen: this comic en-

trance was unintentional. Your guards are a little rough!

Dr. Dish. They're good enough fellows when you get to know them.

Bimbo (*hopefully*). Can they be bribed?

Dr. Dish. Oh, no! They're subjected to a very rigorous discipline.

Bimbo. I see. And what is it you do here?

Dr. Dish. We sift sand.

Bimbo. Ah, you sift sand! Is that interesting?

Dr. Dish. It's not precisely interesting, but one gets used to it.

Bimbo. I should think it would be rather monotonous.

Dr. Dish. It's far less monotonous than shovelling it—after all, there's a progression in sifting. According to the Government's system, they grade the sand-grains in seventy different sizes and for each size we have a separate sieve. First, the smallest grains are sifted out—then, the next smallest, and so on—till there are only the largest left. When the reservoir has been emptied, we are given a holiday. The different grades are used for different purposes.

Bimbo. And about how long does it take to sift out the seventy sizes?

Dr. Dish. That depends: some can do it in a year; others take two or three.

Osbert. But surely you're used to the Desert by this time?

BIMBO. It will take me longer than this to get used to it.

OSBERT. Haven't you already served your term as a shoveller?

BIMBO. No, my dear fellow—I arrived today for the first time. I believe that I heard something said about the shovelling being overmanned and the sifting department short-handed. At any rate, they put me straight in here.

DR. DISH. Yes, the sifting is done by the intellectuals—and the old professional classes—and there are fewer and fewer all the time. This is the intellectual section here. When you've served for five years as a shoveller, if you're found to have the requisite intelligence, you're promoted to be a sifter. But you must have a good character, too—no eccentrics or fanatics are admitted. We are put upon our word of honor—we're less rigorously watched than the shovellers, but we must promise not to try to escape. So I should perhaps let you know at once that your suggestion of bribing the guard was not quite in the best of taste. We are put, as I say, on our honor, and we're allowed to pursue our studies outside our working hours.

BIMBO. I am sorry to have made such a blunder. —And the sand, when it's sifted, I take it, is used in the manufacture of glass for these beautiful glass cities.

OSBERT. You call them beautiful?

BIMBO. I call them ulcers on the crocodile of

Hell!—How the devil did the people of this country ever come to let themselves in for this insane manufacture of glass?

OSBERT. It was Mr. Rudolf's Glass Company: they discovered some new way of making glass cheaply.—Won't you come inside?

They enter the shack as the Doctor goes on talking.

DR. DISH. Mr. Rudolf, the Prince's Prime Minister, bought up all the forests and stone quarries, before anybody knew what he was doing, and then completely stopped work on them. So that he had a monopoly on building materials and was in a position to make people pay four times as much for glass houses as they ever had paid for stone ones! Then he forced the Prince to abdicate and set himself up as Dictator by a coup d'état.—Yet his regime has been highly successful—indeed, his influence, in many ways, has been exceedingly salutary. The old regime was very corrupt. Now we have a much better disciplined government.

BIMBO. Is this where I'm supposed to live?

DR. DISH. They'll put in another cot.

BIMBO. Highly unsafe, these glass houses, I should think.

DR. DISH. Well, they don't burn up, of course— and it was on the strength of that recommendation that the public was first persuaded to accept them. But they are rather easily wrecked in time of war and easily broken into. And they are subject to all sorts of accidents. An explosion in the Government Glass-Works may sometimes destroy a whole town.

BIMBO. Which the Glass Company then has to rebuild!

OSBERT. Some people believe that the Government causes the explosions itself.

BIMBO. Well, the cause of my imprisonment is plain!

DR. DISH. What do you mean?

BIMBO. I was trying to sell axes. I thought they were still chopping down trees.

DR. DISH. Nothing could be more ill-advised!

BIMBO. Well, I have sold French post-cards to the English—German paintings to the French—prayer-books and psalters to the Soviets and harpsichords to the Congo. I have sold all these things and more to the Americans, who will buy anything.

DR. DISH. It was a fatal mistake to come here.

BIMBO. True, the axes I was selling were no good. They worked at first and then they crumbled.

OSBERT. If you explained that to Mr. Rudolf, perhaps he might set you free.

BIMBO. I doubt it: I find the Glass Government excessively stupid and brutal.—Good God! what a change in these years! I, too, gentlemen, am a native of this country—though I left it when I was young. In those days, life was simple; there was a population of only a few thousand; we lived on the edge of the forest. But there was freedom, there was leisure, there was gaiety—there were dances and antelope races. We were the happiest people in the world! And now, when I come back, after many wanderings, I find cities too grim for gaiety and a vast population of slaves content to sift sand in the Desert!

DR. DISH. Well, you know, it is hard to be sure that History does not justify slavery!

BIMBO. A pig's itch upon History! What I act is what History must write!

DR. DISH (*glancing out the window*). And besides, we by no means lack romance—for those who are young enough to enjoy it! (*A knock at the door.*) (*Smiling archly*) Unless I am much mistaken, that is the knock of a very charming lady!

A woman has appeared outside from around the back of the shack and has knocked at the side door. She is a tall dark handsome girl, dressed in green. Osbert goes to open the door.

DR. DISH (*to Bimbo*). I think it might be discreet for you and me to withdraw! Good-evening, Miss Emerald. I have the honor of presenting to you the latest recruit to our company. (*To Bimbo*) I don't think you've told us your name.

BIMBO (*bowing*). Call me Bimbo. (*He kisses her hand.*)

DR. DISH. And I am Dr. Dish and this is Mr. Osbert Rosemary.—(To *Emerald*) I hope you will excuse us. Mr. Bimbo and I are going out for a walk. I want to show him our oasis.

OSBERT. No, really—really: don't go. We'd be delighted to have you stay!

DR. DISH (*smiling*). I want him to see the oasis before nightfall—while the green is still clearly visible.

Dr. Dish and Bimbo take their leave, Dr. Dish smiling benignantly on the young people.

EMERALD. You behave in the presence of other people as if you cared nothing about me! (*Osbert makes no reply.*) You compromise me by having me come here—then you make people think you don't care about me!

OSBERT (*sitting down in a chair beside the table, while Emerald stands upright in the middle of the room*). I don't make you come here. You come of your own accord.

EMERALD. You mustn't say that: you must say, "I'm sorry, dear: I do care for you."

OSBERT (*after a moment's silence*). I'm not going to say anything of the kind.

EMERALD. That's what you're supposed to say: we've been through this scene a thousand times. Now you say, "I'm sorry, dear."

OSBERT. No: I'm tired of saying that.

EMERALD. Osbert: are you insane? You mustn't let me down like that!—This is what comes of not living in the Married Section: you think that you can treat me without respect! (*Osbert is silent.*) Oh, Osbert: why not take me to the Married Section? Then we shouldn't have these quarrels: it would all be so much easier then!

OSBERT. I'm damned if I'll go to the Married Section: it's bad enough as it is!

EMERALD. You compromise me! You neglect me! And now you tell me you won't take me to the Married Section! I thought that was understood!

OSBERT. I tried to leave it very ambiguous.

EMERALD. How can you look yourself in the face.

OSBERT. I don't, except when I have to shave.

EMERALD. That's coarse and caddish to talk like that! And you call yourself a poet! —*Now* you *must* say, "I'm sorry, dear"!

OSBERT. I don't call myself anything: I'm nothing and nobody now!

EMERALD. You're something to me, Osbert.

OSBERT. All right: I'm sorry, dear.

EMERALD. This whole scene's in detestable taste!

OSBERT. I know it, but so is our whole life. So is the sand-sifting camp! So is Mr. Rudolf's Government!

EMERALD. Be careful!

OSBERT. This fellow who came today has made me feel that I'm buried alive. He comes from here, but went away before the glass-manufacturing began. The whole thing fills him with horror.

Dr. Dish and Bimbo have returned, and Dish knocks discreetly at the door.

OSBERT. Come in.

They enter.

DR. DISH. I do hope you'll forgive us for coming back: there seems to be a sandstorm looming.

EMERALD. I'll ask Dr. Dish to take me home, if it isn't too much trouble!

DR. DISH. What? what? a lovers' quarrel?— Plead with her my boy, like a poet!

OSBERT. All my pleadings have been in vain.

EMERALD (*sitting down in the other chair*). I insist upon going at once!

OSBERT. She insists upon going at once.

EMERALD (*brusquely getting up*). *All right!* Come, Dr. Dish!

She takes his arm and they go out.

DR. DISH (*deprecatingly*). Ah, my dear—! (*As they go off, outside the shack*) Would that these old lips were young, to kiss that pretty pout away!

OSBERT (*to Bimbo*). Well, did you enjoy the oasis?

BIMBO (*sitting down in a chair*). I did indeed: charming! charming! That pretty old dented tin cup supplied by the Rudolf Government and chained fast to the crystal spring—what a delightful feature *that* is!

OSBERT. You think it's all unspeakable, don't you?

BIMBO. I was trying just now to find words for it.

OSBERT. Well, it *is* unspeakable! When you live here, no matter how much you try not to, you find yourself getting as hard and as colorless and as nameless as a grain of sand!

BIMBO. But you have your intellectual pursuits?

OSBERT. Intellectual pursuits! When I came to this place, I hoped to be a poet—today I am nothing at all. When I was working among the shovellers, I still kept on writing poetry—I used to publish it under a pseudonym in the *Sand-Shovellers' Gazette*, but the *Gazette* was finally stopped. My poems were revolutionary in those days. Now I almost never write poetry, and when I do, it makes me sick—

> My soul to-day is high as mouldy cheese—
> Its flavor ripened by a million mites—
> Sick stagnant dreams and spent intensities,
> Cold coddled lusts and unexploded spites!

That's the sort of way you get, and you decide you might better be dead!

BIMBO. Well, from my point of view, I confess, the prospect *is* a little unalluring.

Dr. Dish comes back into the shack in time to hear Bimbo's remark.

DR. DISH. And what do you mean, pray, by your point of view?

BIMBO (*dramatically getting up*). I mean the point of view of a citizen of the old free Principality! In the old days before this Glass Government, our country was the happiest in the world.

Prince Louis respected the people and allowed them to do as they pleased, and the people adored the Prince. We settled our own affairs in town meetings so friendly and so informal that we held them in little cafés. We had no particular natural resources except the trees in the forest and so never became very rich—but then, on the other hand, no-body envied us, and our neighbors usually left us in peace. We had no industry except logging; little war; and no revolution; no poverty—and no riches. Our prisons were practically empty, and our lib-eral institutions were our boast. I was a forester, not a man from the towns—and our life in the forests was rough: we built our own houses and killed our own game. But those woodlands were the temples of freedom!—When I tried to revisit the forests just now, I found a high iron fence around them and was told that they were forbidden.

Dr. Dish. That's to keep people from building wooden houses.

Bimbo. To keep them from living like freemen, instead of like spiritless slaves!

Dr. Dish. Do you really believe, my dear sir, that human beings are capable of freedom? I re-member your foresters well—they were disorderly creatures at best, at the mercy of their appetites and passions. Can such persons be said to be free? And had you no wives who blackmailed their hus-bands? No husbands who bullied their wives? no parents who harassed their children? no children

who imposed on their parents? You had the freedom to range in your forests, but had you the freedom to live up to your own ideals? Did your own
natures leave you free? Ah, my dear young fellow,
it is certain that if History teaches us anything, it
is that freedom is a will-o'-the-wisp: we are always
talking about it, but we never manage to attain it
—and we do not even know what we mean by it.
For my part, I will frankly confess that I neither
expect it nor desire it—that I never think about it
at all. Human beings need a master to tell them
what to do, and since some sort of tyranny is inevitable, I prefer a comprehensive and well-admin-
istered one, such as Mr. Rudolf gives us.

BIMBO (*vehemently*). If humanity had wished
such a fate, we should be living like ants in ant-
hills!

DR. DISH. We may learn many things from the
ant: we may envy him even perhaps.

BIMBO. Who in God's name envies an ant?

DR. DISH. Mankind may overrate its importance.

BIMBO. If *we're* not important, who is? If you're
not important, *I* am! God forbid I should stay in
a place where the slaves are defending their slavery!

DR. DISH. I'm afraid you'll find it difficult to go
elsewhere.

BIMBO. I may find it difficult, but I'll go!

DR. DISH. My dear fellow, it has been tried a
thousand times and every time it has proved impossible. This wall has been found unscalable, and

once you got out of the reservation, you would either be shot by a guard or die of thirst in the desert. I once amused myself by writing a history of the attempts to escape which have been made— and I think you will do well to read it before taking any rash action.

BIMBO. God's gullet hawk your history! I'll be gone from here tonight!

OSBERT. I'll go with you!

DR. DISH. Don't be foolhardy, my boy!

OSBERT. I don't care: I'm ashamed to stay!

DR. DISH. Don't let this foolish fellow carry you away! You will be sure to end in disaster.

BIMBO (*going to the window and hauling in the clothes-line, which he detaches*). You'd better not think at all, if you really want to make your getaway!—Or think of that human puma Emerald who was harrying you just now!

DR. DISH. What will the Inspector say, when he finds the clothes-line gone?

BIMBO (*snatching the table-cloth off the table with a single sudden jerk—like a juggler in vaudeville—so that the cutlery and the china still remain in their places*). We won't be here to care! (*To Osbert*) Here: help me with this rope!

They cut the rope into four lengths and tie them to the four corners of the table-cloth, with a large knot at the other end. He makes Osbert tie the rope to the back of his belt.

DR. DISH (*while this is going on*). Remember

that you gave your word of honor!—your word of honor as a man of breeding! Wait till your ten-year term expires!

OSBERT (*stopping*). That's true—I gave my word of honor.

BIMBO (*stuffing bread into his pockets and a bottle of water*). What's your honor against your liberty?

He wraps the parachute around him and buttons his coat over it.

DR. DISH. We shall all be sent back to shovelling!

BIMBO. Not me!

DR. DISH. They'll punish *me* if you escape!

BIMBO. I hope the news may never reach us.— Now, don't let me hear another yap out of you (*he picks up a knife from the table and before putting it in his pocket, holds it up for Dr. Dish to see*) or it'll be the last word on current affairs ever delivered by a distinguished historian!—Stay inside and hold your tongue—say you didn't know what we were doing. Say you were asleep. (*To Osbert*) Now follow me!

They go out. Dr. Dish goes to the door and watches them through the crack.

DR. DISH. How desperate he is, poor fellow!

BIMBO (*affably addressing the Guard, who has just come opposite the shack*). Good evening, sentry.

THE GUARD. Evening, sir.

BIMBO. Sandstorm blew over it seems.

THE GUARD. Yes, it's a lovely calm night. Every star just as plain as a nail!

BIMBO. They move on their rounds like the sentries, eh?—keeping order up in the sky. (*He takes out a cigar and lights it.*)

THE GUARD. I'd hate to have to think that that was all there was to the world!

BIMBO. What do you mean?—Have a cigar?

THE GUARD. We're not allowed to smoke on duty.—Why, just going the rounds. I mean.

BIMBO. Ah, you shouldn't say that, my dear fellow! What can be nobler than to go the rounds? We workers with our brains are keeping order with our supervision just as your guardsmen are with your guns. We patrol our appointed beats just as you do—alert to seize the madman or the rebel who attempts to violate our discipline.—(*Offering him the cigar again and making as if to reach it up*) Take one and smoke it later.

THE GUARD. I'm not supposed to come down.

BIMBO. I don't want to risk throwing it up to you: it might fall down and get broken. It's a Dictator Rudolfo and they're too precious to waste.

THE GUARD. See, sometimes I might lower the ladder and come down just a little ways, when it was somebody I knew, see—but you just came in today and you're not enrolled as a regular yet.

BIMBO. That's true, but I'm a friend of Mr. Rosemary, who will vouch for my good faith. You know Mr. Rosemary, of course. (*Gesturing toward Osbert, who is standing in the shadow of the shack*)

THE GUARD (*noticing him for the first time*). Oh, yes: good-evening, sir.

OSBERT. Good evening, Lemuel.

BIMBO (*passing the cigar to Osbert*). Here, hand this up to him, Berty. (*To the Guard*) Yes, Guard, Mr. Rosemary and I are, like you, among the satellites of the great system that revolves about the Dictator, and we are well content to keep to our beats.

THE GUARD. Then why are you in here?

BIMBO. I'm here as an inside observer.

The Guard lets down a rope-ladder. Osbert comes forward holding up the cigar. The Guard, with his gun in his right hand begins to descend the ladder, holding on with his left hand. Bimbo suddenly jumps and grabs the butt of the gun, which goes off in the air. Between trying to save the gun and trying to hold on to the ladder, the Guard falls to the ground, and Bimbo leaps upon him and stabs him with the table-knife.

BIMBO. Quick! Up the ladder!

He and Osbert climb quickly up and stand on top of the wall, where Bimbo shakes out the parachute.

BIMBO. Quick: climb on my back! (*He crouches down, and Osbert climbs on his back.*)

OSBERT. Poor fellow! He had a touch of the poet!

BIMBO. What's that greenery over there?

OSBERT. Mr. Rudolf's Pleasure-Garden.

BIMBO. Now for the flight of the lark and the eagle!—Ready: go! (*He jumps.*)

DR. DISH (*watching from the shack*). What romanticism!

Two guards, alarmed by the shot, run up from opposite directions along the wall and fire down toward Bimbo and Osbert.

DR. DISH. They will never succeed!

SCENE 2

An open-air pavilion in Mr. Rudolf's Pleasure-Garden, lighted up as if for some gaiety. There is a dancing-floor and, at the right in the foreground, a platform with chairs and music-stands for an orchestra. The walls are lattices, overgrown with various kinds of flowers and with openings at regular intervals. The whole place is paved with moonlight. Distant music is heard from the Casino.

Osbert and Bimbo have just landed outside; the parachute lies beside them on the ground. Bimbo gathers it up and Osbert detaches the ropes from his belt. Bimbo hides it offstage, presumably behind a bush.

BIMBO. What an exhilarating flight! It's lucky we had the wind behind us.

Osbert. Up there we seemed as free as birds soaring over the meadows in summer—how tranquil and gentle the earth looked! Now earth has laid our flight by the heels, and we are challenged by human works.

Bimbo. Where are we?—do you know?

Osbert. Yes: I think I recognize it—it's a sort of open-air ball-room that's near the old Casino.

Bimbo. What? Of course! It used to belong to the Summer Palace. I have danced here a hundred times!—and with the prettiest girl of the season!

Osbert (*looking out through one of the doors*). It reminds me of something, too. The last time I was in a garden and smelt grass and flowers growing—it's five years ago now—I'd gone to meet the girl I was in love with, and she was coming to the city to join me, and we thought we were going to be married—and now I come back an outlaw, and I don't even know where she is!—I suppose we mustn't ever trust life. They supply us with maps at the start, but then there are new roads and they turn out to take us to the wilderness.

A golden and argentine crowing is heard: the sound of the music has ceased.

Bimbo (*apprehensively*). What's that noise?

Osbert. It's such a long time since I've heard it! It's the crowing of the gold and silver pheasants in what used to be Prince Louis's gardens. If they weren't Mr. Rudolf's now, how exquisite their voices would sound! How they would blend with this fragile moonlight and with these odors, acrid and vague! How our shrillest, most passionate purposes would seem to run silvery-thin!

BIMBO. Good Heavens! my dear boy—they've finally got you reduced to a state where you hardly seem to want to act. We'd better get out of these gardens!

OSBERT. Yes: I've been reduced to doubt everything. What's a moment's beauty here? We'll be caught when it's light again—what good will it have been to have acted? It's only the lapsing of life that allows us the illusion of beauty. It's only when we're no longer balked by our being at cross-purposes with others. It's only when the voices of men are still, the roads empty and the houses shuttered —only then may the poet bemuse himself with imaginings of harmony and happiness! (*Composing*):

Bright day dislimns the soul with sights undreamed,
    Dull darkness lightens all through blinded eyes—

BIMBO. For God's sake, stop: you make me nervous!—Do you know exactly where we are?

OSBERT. Right in the middle of the gardens, I'm afraid.

BIMBO. Look out: there's somebody coming!

They hide behind a lattice. Queenie and Lucille enter, dressed as cigarette girls: red aprons and red suspenders over short white dresses:

bobbed hair and little red pill-box hats on one side of their heads; round red spots of rouge on their cheeks.

QUEENIE. Mr. Trixie has been so kind to me: he promised me a pair of brass ear-rings!

LUCILLE. You'd better say you need money.

QUEENIE. But he said they were valuable antiques!

LUCILLE. If they're antiques, they're the kind that aren't valuable. Both those boys are full of meringue.

OSBERT (*stepping out from behind the lattice*). Lucille!

QUEENIE. Oh, Berty!

LUCILLE. Well, for Heaven's sake! Look who's here!

OSBERT. Don't talk too loud: I've escaped from the Desert.

LUCILLE (*smiling*). Well, you've certainly got nerve!

OSBERT. We jumped off the ramparts with a parachute.—But what are *you* doing here?

LUCILLE. Hustling cigarettes.

OSBERT. I was just thinking of you tonight when we landed in the gardens—I thought of that night that I met you in the garden just before I left home. —You must tell me all that's happened to you!

QUEENIE. Oh, I've thought of you always, Berty! I've read your poems over and over! You know that poem you gave Lucille—I pasted it in my memory-book and I've read it over and over!

OSBERT. Why didn't Lucille paste it in *her* memory-book?

QUEENIE. Lucille doesn't keep a memory-book.

BIMBO (*appearing from behind the lattice*). If you will pardon me—I'm a friend of Berty's and a fellow fugitive—our most pressing problem just now is to get away from these gardens.

LUCILLE. There's a big party on tonight and they're checking up on everybody that goes through the gate.

BIMBO. Mr. Rudolf's police won't take bribes?

LUCILLE. No: you better not try to get by them.

BIMBO. And the people submit to this!

LUCILLE. They're beginning to get sore now— everybody hates the police. (*Looking around to see no one is listening*) I hear a lot of talk nowadays that Mr. Rudolf's government may crash!

BIMBO. Crash? Do you mean a revolution?

LUCILLE. There's been a lot of trouble lately over this big Transparency question.

BIMBO. Transparency? What do you mean?

LUCILLE. Mr. Rudolf's got a new idea to have everybody build their houses out of transparent glass instead of the kind you can't see through. It costs extra to glaze them and stain the glass, and the police can't see through the walls.

BIMBO. A very trying state of things, I should—

He stops as two figures come in through one of the forward entrances and stand talking at the front of the stage. They are Trixie and Tiralira. They wear elegant uniforms: Trixie's is a pale violet and Tiralira's a canary yellow.

TIRALIRA. Don't make her expect too much, old boy: don't give her too much at first!

TRIXIE. No Archie, I've been charming with her, but firm. Oh, Archie: you have no idea what this Strength-Suggestion treatment has done for me! I used to be so pliable, so volatile, so shy, so unsure of myself! You remember how easily influenced I was—and how the presence of the opposite sex used to throw me into a state of panic! Well, now that I've submitted to a Psychic Inventory, all my shyness has disappeared: I have become resourceful, steadfast, alert! I've been developing a new artistic boldness in combinations of lavender and orange: my new tea-cosies and sofa-cushions are the most creative things I have ever done.—And now I find that I can interview a glass official without showing a shadow of diffidence—and I believe I can dominate a woman as easily as crush a grape!

QUEENIE (*coming forward*). Oh, Mr. Trixie!

TRIXIE (*starting violently*). Oh, my dear: how you startled me!

QUEENIE. Mr. Trixie, there are two friends of ours here who have been working on the decorations and they haven't got any cards yet. The man who makes the cards out has gone home, and they're afraid that the gate-keeper won't understand and may not let them get out of the gardens. Couldn't you give them a pass so they can get through the gate?

TRIXIE. Oh—well—really I don't know!—

TIRALIRA. Two friends of yours? What are they doing here? How is it they don't have passes?

BIMBO. They forgot to give us any.

TIRALIRA (*aside to Trixie*). I'm afraid that our little friends are trifling with us! (*He comes closer and looks at Bimbo and Osbert.*)

Osbert. Why, Mr. Tiralira!

TIRALIRA. Ah, well, well, my boy—it's you! (*Shaking hands with him cordially*.) How lovely to see you here!—and how unexpected! I thought you were still winning your chevrons among our gallant soldiers of the sands!

BIMBO. They just took us out for the party tonight.

OSBERT. We're supposed to go back now—but if they won't let us through the gate, we'll have to spend the night on the grass.

TIRALIRA. I'm awfully sorry, old boy, but we have no authority to give passes.—Who sent you here.

BIMBO. The Sand-Sifting Director.

TIRALIRA. Come back to the Palace with me, and I'll try to get in touch with him.—It's a rotten shame you should be bothered, and I wish I could do something for you sooner, but with all this anti-

Transparency nonsense, they have to be particularly careful just now about letting people in or out of the gardens.—I suppose you've heard about poor dear Mrs. Megrim?

OSBERT. No: what has happened to her?

TIRALIRA. She broke up on her way to the Spa, and we couldn't do anything but collect the pieces. But I've had her put together and beautifully mounted for Mr. Rudolf's museum.

Two figures enter from the right. Tiralira, seeing them, and stretching out his arms on each side, makes Osbert and Bimbo fall back behind the lattice and motions Trixie to fall back into a doorway; he himself remains looking through the doorway in such a way as not to be seen by the newcomers, and listens to their conversation. The two men are obviously officials, but one wears a red business suit, an orange derby and a fine blond mustache, while the other has a coarse dark mustache and plain dark clothes. They are the Head Stainer and the Head Glazer of Mr. Rudolf's Glass Government.

THE HEAD STAINER (*nervously, taking out his watch*). It's almost five minutes past twelve.

THE HEAD GLAZER. Don't get nervous—wait for the flare.

THE HEAD STAINER. What time have you got, Head Glazer?

THE HEAD GLAZER. I don't know. Don't worry —we'll see the flare.

THE HEAD STAINER. Suppose Mr. Rudolf should suspect something and refuse to leave the Palace.

THE HEAD GLAZER. He won't, though—don't worry, Stainer. He'd never suspect the Admiral. Old Flogger will make him walk in the gardens on the pretext of discussing the new gunboats, and as soon as they're behind the big fountain, our men will gag Mr. Rudolf, pop him into an old fertilizer sack and push him away in a wheelbarrow. In the meantime, the Palace Guards will have taken the Summer Palace and the Capitol. The people will support the revolution—in fact, they're more than half expecting it.

THE HEAD STAINER. What a day of joy for the people, Glazer! Their right to live in privacy again! And their right to revel in color! They shall have more brilliant color than they ever have dreamed of!

THE HEAD GLAZER. The only thing that worries me now, Stainer, is—suppose Mr. Rudolf's supporters cause trouble—you and I may have to make speeches to the people—and we're craftsmen, not politicians. Mr. Rudolf's banished all the politicians who didn't support the Glass Government. What we need is a political spellbinder—

The music suddenly stops.

THE HEAD STAINER. There! the music has stopped!

A red flare lights up at the back of the stage.

TIRALIRA (*to Trixie*). They've set out to overthrow the government! That's the Head Stainer and the Head Glazer.

Trixie. My goodness! hadn't we better get away! They may shoot us for being loyal to Mr. Rudolf!

Tiralira. Are we all that loyal, old boy? Where will your color combinations be if the edict against color is issued and you can only do sofa-cushions for the Palace?—Don't run: we're as well off here as anywhere.

Shouts and cheers have been heard, drawing nearer. A detachment of Guards appears from the left, marching in twos. The Captain salutes the Stainer and the Glazer, who have mounted on the platform to the right. They return the salute, touching their derbies.

The Captain of the Guards. The Palace, sir, has been taken. Mr. Rudolf is under arrest. I hereby put off the Iron Pansy of Mr. Rudolf's Glass Government and declare my allegiance to the Government of Glazed and Colored Glass.

He strips the Iron Pansy from the right side of his breast, and the other Guards do the same. They throw them to the ground with a loud clang of hardware.

The Captain. Long live Stainer and Glazer!

The Guards. Long live Stainer and Glazer!

In the course of this scene and the scene that follows, Rudolf's revellers drift in. Some are outrageously ugly, others grotesquely deformed; some have half-witted faces, or lack eyes, nose or mouth. All are, however, dressed correctly in evening clothes. The only normal-looking persons among them are a young man and his young wife: she is pretty and demure, he wears round bone-rimmed spectacles and carries a piece of lead pipe. There are two large birds and a bear, all in uniform. Waiters mingle with the crowd.

GLAZER. Mr. Rudolf's Government has surrendered. The country will be run in the future by the Government of Stainers and Glazers. We usher in a new period of prosperity. Hereafter every house will be glazed.—

Some cheering among the crowd, and one wild and crazy guffaw.

GLAZER (*turning to the Stainer*). You'd better talk to them—you've got more of a gift of gab than I have.—(*Turning to the crowd*) Fellow-citizens, the Head Stainer will address you. He will outline to you more eloquently than I can the new policies and programs of our Government.

STAINER (*addressing the crowd with sincere enthusiasm and feeling*). Fellow citizens! Fellow glass-house-dwellers! This is a day for thanksgiving and rejoicing. We had been threatened by Mr. Rudolf's Government with the loss of our right to live in privacy and with the loss of our right to color. But tonight Mr. Rudolf's Government has fallen and these rights are once again secure! (*Some cheering*) Why, color! My Fellow-Citizens—think of a world deprived of color!—as, save for the officials

in their uniforms, we were well on our way to becoming. The colors!—we inherit them with life
itself, with the light that lifts us out of the slime.
They are the riches, the inexhaustible treasury,
which are brought us by the rays of the sun—
Red! Orange! Yellow! Green! Blue! Purple!
Violet!—the Blessed Mystic Seven of the Spectrum! Why, without the right to build and dress in
color—with all the houses transparent and colorless,
and all the clothing gray—how should we have
answered the summons of the light? We should
have been more wretched than the lowest golden
beetle, more sickly than the commonest rosy-
breasted bird! Every match that we scratched
would have mocked us with its red and yellow
flame!—every dewdrop would have put us to
shame! We should have gone mad with sullenness
and sadness for never having answered the light!
And now with the definite defeat of Mr. Rudolf's
dull and sullen government, we shall be free to
speak the language of the sun: Red! Orange! Yellow! Green! Blue! Purple! Violet! And all the
colors that lie between or which the cunning of
man may combine—bright sapphires and canaries
and vermilions! rich heliotropes and sepias and
maroons!—Dahlia-Purple! Shrimp-Pink and Rose-
Opal! Electric-Blue and Peacock-Green! Poppy-
Red! Coxcomb-Red! Oxblood-Red!! Claret-lees
Red!!!

Hoots and squawks from the crowd, insane laughter.

OSBERT (*to Lucille*). Who are all those awful creatures?

LUCILLE. They're Mr. Rudolf's retinue: his councillors and officials.

OSBERT. I already had a low opinion of Rudolf, but I'm surprised at his having that bear.

LUCILLE. He's not so bad when you get to know him.

OSBERT. Mr. Rudolf?

LUCILLE. No, I mean the bear.

Glazer has laid a hand on the Stainer's arm as the latter was about to continue his speech.

THE GLAZER. Listen here: go easy on that color stuff. After all, they don't need color to keep their houses from being seen into. We can talk about color later. The main thing to give them is glazing.

STAINER (*fervent and indignant*). I will never allow the people to be deprived of the sacred spectrum!

Excited and adverse murmurs on the part of the crowd.

THE CAPTAIN (*who has posted his men at the back of the stage*). Somebody had better say something to them. We don't want to use violence, if we can help it. And we don't want to let this bunch get out of hand: some of them have got nasty teeth and claws.

Bimbo has made his way through the crowd

*from the other side of the stage and, coming up
on the platform behind them, addresses Glazer
and Stainer.*

BIMBO. Gentlemen: allow me to present myself!
I am a citizen of the old free Principality and a
fugitive from Mr. Rudolf's Government. I was
considered something of an orator in the old days,
when oratory was still cultivated in this country—
and, if you'd permit me, I'd be delighted to say a
word or two to this crowd in behalf of our free
institutions. You are great statesmen, Mr. Stainer
and Mr. Glazer—you are incomparable executives,
but you are unskilled in the arts of the public
speaker, and for the lack of the proper words at
this crisis, you may find yourselves in unnecessary
difficulties. I have been a politician as well as a sales-
man—it's more or less the same thing.

GLAZER (*somewhat rattled, to Stainer*). Can we
trust him?

BIMBO (*addressing the assembly*). Fellow-Citizens: I come before you to announce the victory
of liberty and justice—the vindication of those free
institutions which are our heritage, our glory and
our pride! A great insult, Fellow-Citizens, has been
offered to our traditional liberties—a great crime
against them has been attempted! It had been pro-
posed by the former ruler to deprive our people of
their privacy—to take away the decent protection
of their houses and to expose them naked and
shameless—to throw thousands of them out of work.

But, fortunately, champions of the people were found—true men of action, true leaders, true prophets—to call for an accounting—to sound a clarion-call—and to strike a decisive blow: Mr. Glazer and Mr. Stainer! And the men of the National Guard have arisen to a man to answer that call and to stand behind that knock-out blow! Hereafter the Stainers' and Glazers' Government will see to it that the houses of the people are well glazed and stained with bright color as houses should be glazed and stained!

The Guards and the waiters cheer, but the creatures hoot and murmur ominously.

THE CAPTAIN (*to Bimbo*). Don't talk too much about the people's rights. Some of these people are heads of departments and the regulations don't affect them—they're only afraid of losing their jobs.

BIMBO. Right you are! (*He turns to the audience.*) Some of you loyal citizens here may dread a change of government. That is a very natural feeling and a very sound feeling—but let me hasten to allay your apprehensions. Though the government has changed hands, the economic structure will not suffer. Not a wheel will cease from turning, not a screw will be loosed from its place, in the majestic machine of the Glass Government! You know Mr. Glazer and Mr. Stainer for the responsible public servants they are. I see among you some heads of government departments, and such men will not need to

be told that the interests of the Glazers and the
Stainers are identical with your own. If they quarrel with the policy of the last government, it is
partly because they believe that, under Mr. Rudolf's regime, the officials of the Glass Government
received very much less than their due. Fellow-
Citizens, for a quarter of a century Mr. Rudolf has
been growing rich at our expense. Not only has he
barely allowed the people a living wage, he has
prevented the holders of public office—men at least
as industrious, as able, as indispensable as he—from
sharing in the recent profits. While the people have
dressed in the coarsest clothes and eaten unwhitened
bread—while the public officials themselves, the
mainstays and helmsmen of our commonwealth,
have been forced to live on pitifully limited in-
comes—Mr. Rudolf has arrayed himself in gold-
leaf and has eaten gardenia salad. While the rest of
us have been sifting and shovelling sand—or per-
forming arduous administrative duties—Mr. Rudolf
has occupied his leisure by racing mechanical antelopes! Fellow-Citizens: we Stainers and Glazers
believe that there is no reason on earth why every
man in this country—nay, why every woman and
child—should not clothe himself in gold-leaf and
eat gardenia salad, too. And in the new era of pro-
ductivity and plenty there is no reason why our be-
loved children should not have mechanical antelopes
to play with!

 Cheering; the birds squawk; the bear growls.

BIMBO (*to the Glazer*). That fetches 'em, you see!

Tiralira bustles up to the platform and gives a hand each to Stainer and Glazer.

TIRALIRA. Gentlemen, I congratulate you! I salute the new regime! I shall circulate among the guests and do what I can to reassure them. A tactful word here and there might be useful in making things smoother.

He mingles with the crowd and is seen hurrying from one to another, holding the women's hands, putting his arm around the men's shoulders, earnestly and vivaciously conversing with them.

A NOSELESS MAN IN THE CROWD. What about the tariff?

BIMBO. The new government will protect home industries and at the same time preserve the advantages of free trade.

Applause.

A MEGALOCEPHALIC DWARF. What about the national debt?

BIMBO. The new government will pay it immediately by exporting sand abroad.

Applause as before. Bimbo tries to go on speaking, but the Birds begin to squawk so loudly that he cannot make himself heard.

BIMBO (*to the Captain of the Guard*). Can't those confounded birds be kept quiet?

THE CAPTAIN. We can't afford to offend them. They're very prominent in public affairs.

AN ARMLESS MAN. What about the mutilated glass-workers?

BIMBO. They will be supported at the expense of the city, but without increasing the taxes.

A WOMAN (*who looks like a bird*). What about the rights of birds and animals?

The Birds screech; the Bear comes up to the platform, stands on his hind legs and wildly howls.

BIMBO. The new government will be partly elective, and we want it clearly understood that the voice of every animal and the voice of every bird—of whatever size, species or sex—will have its weight in the common councils!—(*In the course of this speech, the Bear has been sniffing at Bimbo's ankles, and the speaker now turns to the Captain.*) This bear is a little overwrought. I don't think it understands what is being said.

THE CAPTAIN. It's the young fellow with the lead-pipe that's dangerous. You'd better keep your eye on *him*. I'm watching my chance to get it away from him without making trouble.

BIMBO. I believe that some music would be effective at this point. Haven't you got a band that could play something patriotic?

THE CAPTAIN. A good idea! I'll have them here right away. (*He dispatches one of the Guards.*)

THE YOUNG MAN WITH THE LEAD-PIPE (*to Os-*

bert). What an amazing gift of eloquence your friend has.

HIS WIFE. Yes: we think he's the most exciting speaker we've ever heard!

OSBERT. He's a patriot of the old-fashioned type.

THE YOUNG MAN (*candid, good-humored, holding the lead-pipe in one hand and tapping it gently in the palm of the other*). I've always worked for Mr. Rudolf, of course—and I'm sorry to hear him given a bad character—which I can assure you he doesn't deserve—but I think that your friend is a magnificent orator.

Tiralira, in the course of his rounds, comes between the young man and his wife and familiarly takes each by the arm.

THE YOUNG MAN. Oh, Tiralira! What luck! I was just wishing I could ask your advice. I wanted to inquire your attitude toward this movement. I trust your judgment so much and I'm trying to form an opinion.

MR. TIRALIRA. I really haven't been able to form an opinion myself, old boy—but I think it's important to keep people quiet.

THE YOUNG MAN. Yes, of course—you're entirely right, and if there was ever an occasion in the world when your tact and social charm were needed—

TIRALIRA. Don't be silly, old boy—I'm the most bungling person alive!

He turns to go, and the Young Man swiftly

clubs him with the lead-pipe. Tiralira drops; the Young Man and his wife slip away.

TRIXIE. Help! Help! Archie has been assassinated!

Confusion: a group gathers around. Bimbo seizes the opportunity, while the general attention is diverted, to take a gun from one of the Guards and shoot the Bear, which falls dead beside the platform. This increases the disturbance in the crowd. The Young Man with the Lead-Pipe reappears.

THE YOUNG MAN. This bear has been executed without a trial! Ladies and Gentlemen, a valued public servant has been shot down without a hearing! Are we to submit to a Reign of Terror?

Sounds of indignation. At a signal from the Captain, the Guards seize the Young Man, wrest away his lead-pipe and carry him off the scene. His Wife produces a revolver and shoots at the revolutionary leaders, making a hole in Bimbo's derby, which he takes off and coolly examines. The Guards seize her and bundle her off.

BIMBO. Men and Women of the Free Principality! Let there be no more acts of violence! The new government was not the first to use violence —but since violence has been attempted, we must meet violence with violence! Any person who offers resistance will be arrested and held for high treason. The punishment for treason is death. Do not imitate this foolish bear, who, however much we may have loved him and admired his rugged

and loyal nature, must be admitted at a time like
this to have been dangerous to the general welfare,
since his grasp of human language was so far less than
perfect that he was not able to comprehend the
benefits which the new Glazers' and Stainers' order was bringing him. But *you* are responsible and
enlightened citizens, who will settle down and be
at home with a responsible enlightened government!—

An Hydroptic. That Bear understood what was
said to him just as good as a man!

A Cretin. Aw, what're you talkin' about? He
couldn't do nothin' as good as a man!

Bimbo. The National Military Band has arrived.
Freedom and prosperity have triumphed! Let us
celebrate the dawn of a new era!

The band strikes up a march: there are cries of
"Long live the Stainers and Glazers!"

*Mrs. Rosemary appears among the crowd and
is evidently looking for someone. When she
comes near the platform, she cries out in amaze-
ment as she recognizes Bimbo.*

Mrs. Rosemary. Belisarius!

Bimbo. Marguerite!

Mrs. Rosemary. Why, what are you doing here?

Bimbo. I came back to find you, my darling! (*He
embraces her.*) It is just thirty years ago that we
danced in this very pavilion!

Osbert (*recognizing his mother*). Mother!

Mrs. Rosemary. And Osbert, my boy, too!—I

had come to intercede with the government to get
you released from the Desert.

BIMBO. Mr. Rudolf has been overthrown: a new
and liberal regime has begun.

MRS. ROSEMARY. Yes: I have heard about it. The
Head Stainer is a cousin of mine. He was the only
one of our family who succeeded under Mr. Rudolf, and I had come to appeal to him about Osbert.
—Belisarius: this is your son. Osbert: this is your
father! I told you that he was dead because I was
ashamed of his having left me. And I took the name
of Rosemary to make me forget his. I tried to fill
my heart with you and with tying pink ribbons on
the furniture, but somehow it was never enough.

OSBERT. Bimbo my father!

BIMBO. Don't be horrified, my boy. Don't be
ashamed of the old adventurer. If it had not been
for an old rogue like me, the indiscretion might
never have been committed which brought into the
world a poet like you. I may have been selling phony
axes while you were writing magnificent poetry,
but if it hadn't been for my trickery and my brass,
you might never have escaped from the Desert.

MRS. ROSEMARY (*who has been talking with the
Stainer*). This is your Cousin Clarence, Osbert—
and this, Clarence, is my husband.

STAINER. You must stay with us and help us with
our task.

BIMBO. And you shall be Poet Laureate, Osbert!

OSBERT. Lucille: will you marry me?

Lucille (*grinning*). Do you still love me?

Osbert. I never ceased to dream about you all the time I was in the Desert. And now that I am free, you and I can at last live the life of beauty and adventure and romance that we used to imagine as children. We will show these wretched people how to live. My cousin Clarence will cause the towns to bloom like tulips and dahlias, and I, with my poems, shall revive our people's spirit! At last, we shall show the world a civilization where the rulers are artists and poets!

Queenie. Oh, it's all so wonderful, Berty! I always knew we'd see you again!

The Creatures have begun to dance. Mrs. Rosemary is dancing with Bimbo.

Lucille. Come on: dance with me, Berty!

ACT III

The Dictator's office and its anteroom, in the Dictator's palace. The office is on the left and occupies about three-quarters of the stage: it is partitioned off from the anteroom by a wall with an interconnecting door. There are a large desk at the left with an executive's chair for the Dictator and another chair for visitors, a window in the back wall and, between the desk and the window, a door which leads into the Palace. The room had originally been furnished in a semi-regal manner, but has now certain touches inspired by the memory of Mrs. Rosemary's house in Act I: large pink bows on the curtains and a bunch of roses on the desk. In the anteroom at the right, a man in leather overalls—evidently a workman—is sitting: he is gaunt and appears morose. As soon as the curtain has risen, a page in a rose-pink uniform ushers in a second visitor through a door in the right-hand wall. The newcomer is a man of gigantic stature, with hair that sticks straight up on his head and large glaring eyes—he wears high boots, corduroy breeches and a leather packet. He takes a seat next to the man in the overalls.

THE PAGE. Wait here: His Excellency will see you.

THE MAN IN THE BOOTS (*to the man in the overalls, after eyeing him a minute*). Glass-worker?

THE WORKER. Glass-marble worker.

THE MAN IN THE BOOTS. You've come about the riots, eh?

THE WORKER. Yeah. (*After a moment*) What kind of clothes are those you've got on?

THE MAN IN THE BOOTS (*with pride*). I'm a forester. This is the way we dress.

THE WORKER. You don't say. So you're one of those foresters! Well, that's a way out, I suppose. But I hear that they're going to raise hell with you, the same as they have with us.

THE FORESTER. They've served an ultimatum on us, and I've come to talk to Mr. Osbert. I believe he's always been a liberal, and I don't think he can really be against us.

THE WORKER. Liberal? The marble-workers are starving while the Dictator sits in his palace and wears gold-leaf and eats gardenia salad!—And what's the use of going into the forests? They wouldn't be big enough to hold us all, even if they let us stay there. Sooner or later it's got to come to a show-down—

The Forester holds up a warning finger, as he hears the sound of a bell from the next room. While the Marble-Worker has been talking, Osbert has entered his office from the door that leads into the Palace. He wears spectacles and a gilded robe. He examines the papers on his desk, then rings a bell on the desk. The Forester and the Marble-Worker continue their conversation in low voices.

OSBERT. Is the marble-worker here?

THE PAGE. Yes, Your Excellency.

Queenie comes into the office from the Palace. She is a matronly woman now.

QUEENIE (*laying a large scrap-book on the desk*). I've brought you a surprise, Berty!

OSBERT. Why, what's this? (*Opening the book*) My old poems—good heavens!

QUEENIE. I went through all the files of the old papers and cut them out and pasted them in!

OSBERT. How sweet of you! (*Turning over the pages*) What awful rubbish, though! I haven't thought about it for years.

QUEENIE. Oh, no, Berty!—some of them are really splendid—I was quite thrilled when I read them again.

OSBERT. You've even got the stuff I used to write to Lucille.

QUEENIE. Yes: I kept it all in my memory-book.

The Page comes in.

OSBERT (*kissing her*). Thank you very much, my dear—I'll look through it later on. I must attend to business now.

QUEENIE. Don't stay beyond lunch-time, Osbert.

You know that it gives you a headache to work on an empty stomach.

OSBERT. Yes, dear: now you must go. I've got a lot of people to see, and I'm late for my appointments as it is.

She kisses him again and goes out.

OSBERT (*to the Page*). Have the marble-worker come in.

THE PAGE. Yes, Your Excellency.

The Marble-Worker enters.

OSBERT (*shaking hands with him cordially*). How do you do. Sit down, won't you?

THE WORKER. I'm sorry to come in my overalls, sir—but it's the only clothes that I've got.

OSBERT. Are you so badly off as that?

THE WORKER. That is what we were rioting about.

OSBERT. I wish you would tell me exactly what's been happening. I'm new at this job, you know, and don't always know what's what.

THE WORKER. Five hundred glass-marble workers have been thown out of work and they're starving—that's what's been happening, Mr. Osbert.

OSBERT. Mr. Megim informed me two weeks ago that he had offered employment on his place to all the men who have been thrown out of work.

THE WORKER. Mr. Megrim has a big place, but he can hardly use five hundred workers.

OSBERT. It seems to me your attitude toward

Mr. Megrim hasn't been a very patient or tactful one—when you break the windows of his aviary and allow his valuable birds to escape.

THE WORKER. It was two months before we did that—in the meantime we'd been dying of hunger and cold.

OSBERT. I didn't know that things were as bad as that.

THE WORKER. That's why I'm here to tell you.

OSBERT. I'll have an investigation made at once, and if conditions are as serious as you say, I'll have adequate relief provided.

THE WORKER. Why not get somebody else to manage the Glass-Marble industry? Almost anybody could run it better.

OSBERT. But who else has Mr. Megrim's experience? There's probably nobody else in the world who understands marble-making as he does.

THE WORKER. I understand that Megrim's a friend of yours, and if that's so, you must realize that he's not a business man. He may know a lot about designing marbles, but as a business man, he's a good owl-fancier—and while Megrim's busy breeding owls, his employees can't breed human beings!

OSBERT. Harry Megrim is an old friend of mine, and it is true that he belongs to the old regime—so that it's true that he's a little impractical because he's idealistic.—But let me tell you precisely what happened. At the time of Mr. Rudolf's dictatorship,

Mr. Rudolf, knowing Harry was fond of owls, appointed him to a post in his aviary. But as Harry's favorite owls came to die, he used to get them stuffed, and he thus became interested in taxidermy. He used to go to the department of the glass-works where the glass eyes were made and have glass eyes especially designed for his owls. The effects were often startling and weird: he has always had an original turn of mind. My father, Mr. Bimbo, when he came to succeed Mr. Rudolf, with a characteristically generous gesture, put Harry in charge of the glass-eye department. Nobody then dreamed that it would ever become important. But Harry began designing children's marbles—they are, of course, very much like glass-eyes. Then playing with children's marbles became a great fad for grown-ups—and Harry Megrim, without having intended it, and, in fact, very much to his surprise, suddenly found himself at the head of a successful business!—

THE WORKER. And how long was the business successful?—There's nothing to the marble business, Mr. Osbert—only children really care about marbles. The whole demand for marble-playing by adults was worked up by that advertizing man. It lasted for a year and a half—then it began to dawn on the public that they didn't really want to play marbles the way the ads said they did. And there was Megrim's making millions of marbles which nobody would ever buy—and then there was half the plant shut down and us marble-workers out of luck!

Osbert. I'm sorry about that, as I've told you, and I'll see to it that something is done. I'm very grateful to you for coming here and telling me exactly what's wrong. But I must ask you not to make things hard for Harry. Such rioting as you have been doing will not, of course, in any case, be tolerated by the government—but even aside from that, I can assure you that it may prejudice Harry against giving you work on his place. He is a shy and sensitive man, and any violent action on your part may put him out of sympathy with you, but if you make him feel that *you* are sympathetic with *him* and ready to coöperate with him, you will find him, I think, kind and humane. And remember that he has only one arm.

Osbert rises, and the visitor rises.

The Worker. Well, kind and humane or not, he certainly ought to be checked on! I understand that his advertizing man's persuaded him that there might be a booming market for glass eyes in the top of pincushions.

Osbert (*smiling*). Well, they might be very charming, mightn't they? Of course, there'd be a face behind them.

The Worker. It doesn't make any sense. Glass-eyed pincushions would give me the willies.

Osbert (*shaking hands*). You'll excuse me if I must break off now—I have still two other people this morning. Thank you very much for coming. Goodby.

The Worker goes out. Osbert rings the bell for the Page and consults a list on the desk.

OSBERT (*as the Page appears*). Is the forester there?

THE PAGE. Yes, Your Excellency.

OSBERT. Have him come in.

He adopts toward the Forester, when he enters, a curter and more peremptory manner.

OSBERT. Sit down, please. (*The Forester sits down.*) Well, it seems, sir, that you people are determined to defy the rulings of the Government!

THE FORESTER. What harm does it do the Government for a few hundred men to live in the forest?

OSBERT. At first it was a few dozen. My father didn't interfere with that. Today it is several thousand, who are becoming a threat to the State. To allow people to go freely to the forests and to build themselves wooden houses is to allow our society to be undermined, attacked in its very foundations. Sooner or later I should have to meet the issue—I should have to oppose your renegades, and I prefer to take a stand now, before it comes down to bloodshed. You have already had the Government's ultimatum, and I can only repeat it to you. If you and your people will move out of the forest at once—your houses will have to be destroyed

—the Government will be perfectly satisfied, and find you employment in the glass works.

THE FORESTER. With these unemployment riots going on? Why not send the unemployed to the forests? There is still room for many more. And it's possible to plant more forests. There's a kind of waste on the other side, but the waste is not too sandy for cultivation.

OSBERT. They couldn't adapt themselves to your wild kind of life, and I am assured that such a policy would be economically unsound.

THE FORESTER. Tell me, if you please, Mr. Osbert, why shouldn't people live in wooden houses? They're much safer and much more comfortable than glass ones.

OSBERT. You must know as well as I do that we are forced to be a glass-manufacturing country. Our whole prosperity is based on glass. We have vast deserts, but very few forests, and the quarries were exhausted years ago.

THE FORESTER. The people got along all right with wood and stone before the forests and the quarries were bought up by Mr. Rudolf so that he could make his millions out of glass.

OSBERT. But we had then a tiny population, hardly five percent of the present one—a mere scattering of villages and country estates along the seaward fringe of the Desert. That society had its distinction and its charm—I used to know it and should be the last to belittle it—but we cannot have it back now if we would. We must keep a tight grasp on our present realities. In our modern world, it is glass which has given our country the power to develop from a little patch hardly visible on the map to a country of tenth-rate importance. By a series of audacious conquests under my father, Mr. Bimbo's leadership, we have extended our glass civilization many kilometers along the shore, and it is glass and glass alone which feeds and clothes our two million people!

THE FORESTER. Mr. Osbert, I have always believed in you, considered you a liberal intelligent man. And I have tried to convince my fellow foresters that when you came to the dictatorship, we should not any longer be hounded.

OSBERT. The most intelligent and salutary thing I can do is to prevent you felling timber for houses.

The Forester's eye falls on the scrapbook of Osbert's poems, which has been left open on the desk.

THE FORESTER. What an irony to find on your desk the very poems which so moved me in my youth!—the very poems which—

OSBERT. That old stuff of mine is horribly bad. At least it's horribly dated. I'm sorry to hear you admired it.

THE FORESTER. I mean Luke Bronkus's poems—you have them here in this book —

OSBERT. I used to write under the name of Luke Bronkus in the days of the censorship.

THE FORESTER. What—*you* wrote the poems signed Luke Bronkus?—those cries of indignation and revolt! It was those poems that first spurred my spirit to rebel against Mr. Rudolf—and then, later, to rebel against the glass civilization and to break away to the woods!

"Rise from your sands, O slaves!—The sun still flees the East—
    Turn not toward darkness yet—the bones of toil are strong!"

OSBERT. That was a phase that I quickly got over—

THE FORESTER (*much excited*). Why, sir, it was that poetry of yours which first kindled in me the spark of hope! I was a sullen soldier of the Desert, living amidst brutality and ignorance, lounging loutishly in my barracks by day, patrolling the ramparts at night, keeping watch over my miserable prisoners and just as much a prisoner as they were. But when I read that great diary of the spirit of yours, when I found out that there was another man like me who could not accept the Desert and the prison—then I plucked up courage to put my faith in the vision of human dignity and freedom:

    "What man has bound his brother may unbind!"

OSBERT. That was a message that may have been needed then when the glass-workers were actually imprisoned, but, as you know, my father changed all that. They now come and go as they please.

THE FORESTER. But they're not able to leave the country and they can't work at anything but glass—and that you, sir, should be head of a government that imposes on them such restrictions!

OSBERT. That movement, of course, was quite justified. My father and my cousin Clarence relieved us of that vulgar tyranny. My cousin stained the houses with beautiful colors—

THE FORESTER. Only for those who could pay for them.

OSBERT. My father threw out cretins from public office—

THE FORESTER. And installed a lot of grafters.

OSBERT. He shortened the workers' hours and paid them regular wages.

THE FORESTER. But made them still work at glass.

OSBERT. There's no way of getting around that. Even before the Revolution, while I was still a prisoner in the Desert, I had had to accept the fact that a glass civilization was inevitable.

FORESTER. Inevitable to live in these hard little cells so brittle that any jar can crack them?

OSBERT. Yes: our glass-making *is* rather old-fashioned.

FORESTER. This makes people very nervous, and yet they're hardly alive. In the forest, we're not nervous—though, of course, we have to be on our guard against the bears and the panthers. Those bears who used to be in uniform are now a degenerate stock and of course are extremely treacherous. But the beasts are at least alive, not like these half-dead people. The trees are alive and the thickets are alive. The animals we shoot are alive, and we nourish our lives from theirs. We don't have to live on the vegetables that you glass people grow under glass. The very beams and planking of our houses are veined with the veinings of life. You have the advantage here of the old stone and wooden Palace. You don't know how the other people live.

OSBERT. Let me tell you I've lived in a stone house, and it was just as inorganic as glass.

THE FORESTER. So did I for that matter. I was the black sheep of a stone-house family. The stone didn't crack, to be sure—but it did restrict my freedom. You can't live in such a coffin of a world.

OSBERT. Yes: I know what you mean.

THE FORESTER. I think we're related through the Grimsons.

OSBERT. How?

THE FORESTER. Henrietta Grimson—she married Guy Hunter. She wrote poetry, you know.

OSBERT. But not very good poetry.

THE FORESTER. Her death was tragic.

OSBERT. Yes.

A knock at the back door.

OSBERT. Come in.

THE PAGE. Some very queer gentlemen to see you.

OSBERT. (*looks at his list*). Mr. Schenck?

THE PAGE. Yes: but very queer gentlemen with him.

OSBERT. Tell him to come by himself.

THE FORESTER. Please think about what I've said.

Osbert is silent. The Forester goes. The Page shows Schenck into the anteroom. He is the Emissary of Act I: spare, sharp-nosed and black-mustached, but now graying. Osbert opens the door.

OSBERT. Please come in.

Schenck enters. They shake hands.

OSBERT. How do you do. Sit down. I was very much interested to hear about your experiments. I take a special interest in biology. What the world needs is better people.

SCHENCK. That's what I'm working on.

OSBERT. Really? You didn't explain in your letter.

SCHENCK. I thought it would be better to see you. I don't want it given publicity yet, and I wanted you to hear the news first—not only on account of your position, but because it was something you said that started me off on the work in the first place.

OSBERT. Something I said?

SCHENCK. You wouldn't remember, but I saw you once years ago. It was under Mr. Rudolf's

government. I'd been given a job serving notice
on people—they were always serving notice then.
I had to crack down on a family who were operating a paperweight factory independently of the
Central Glass Works, and you were there at the
moment and made a rebellious speech: you said
that the work you did, you did for its own sake,
and that the things you made would be alive, and
that you wouldn't work for Mr. Rudolf. Of
course, they couldn't have that kind of talk then,
and they sent you to the Great Desert. But I'd
never heard such defiance, and I couldn't get it out
of my head.

OSBERT. You, too!

SCHENCK. I was interested in biochemistry and,
after I got a good job in the Glass Works, I worked
at it on the side. When your father got to be
Dictator, and things eased up a bit, I'd saved
enough money to drop my job and take a little
house on the shore, where I was able to experiment
with fish-eggs, and it wasn't very long before I found
that I could stimulate them artificially and hatch
out almost any kind of fish. Then I began working
with rats' ova. That was quite a jump, but at the
end of five or six years, I found that I could
fertilize them artificially—not the way they do
with cattle, but with spermatazoa that I synthe-
sized myself.

OSBERT. You made synthetic spermatazoa?

SCHENCK. Better than the rats could themselves,

and I could turn out better rats. I hadn't been able
to find out yet how to control the pigmentation,
so they were sometimes a little spotty, but otherwise my rats were superrats. They got so smart—
I was specializing for brains—that I couldn't keep
them shut in their cages. They'd pull out the nails
and pick the locks and run away. Then come back
and rob the house. So I thought I'd try some other
animal. A rat doesn't give you much of a basis
to work on—from the point of view of character,
I mean. I did some work for a while with dogs, but
the different breeds make things confusing, and
monkeys was where I made the most progress. I
grew some gibbons as big as gorillas, but then,
when I laid off size and concentrated on brains
again, I found that one of my young gibbons was
beginning to talk the local dialect, and I thought
that it was not worth while to try to develop apes
when human beings in certain ways were already
so much further developed. I had only fair success
at first.

OSBERT. But how did you persuade the women
to submit themselves to your experiments?

SCHENCK. Oh, by that time it was all ectogenetic.
The fishermen out there are poor, and the wives
would let me take out one ovary for fifteen zukors
or so. Well, as I say, I made slow progress at first.
Human beings are more complex than most other
animals—and, besides, when they don't come out
right, the results look a lot worse because you can't

help comparing them with other human beings. I won't say that I didn't have some bad miscarriages: giantism, underdevelopment, too many or too few of one organ or limb or another, skeletons that didn't harden. But at last I got what I was after: a human being that's both stronger and smarter.

OSBERT. I'm truly astonished, Mr. Schenck. I've had no idea that such results were possible.

SCHENCK. You people only concentrate on glass and finding serums for the desert diseases. If you would only train some bio-chemists, what a different kind of world we might make!

OSBERT. Could you allow me to see some of your —creations?

SCHENCK. I've got two in the car outside.

OSBERT. Bring them in.

SCHENCK. I don't want them seen yet by anybody except you. I'm afraid they'll attract attention —though I'm afraid your page got a glimpse of them.

OSBERT. Yes: I see. I'll go out with you then.

They rise.

SCHENCK. You'll see that their coloring isn't all that it ought to be—I haven't got the hang of the pigment. Some of the brightest ones are albinos. But I don't think that really matters.

They go out through the anteroom.

Just as the door into the house is closing behind them, Tiralira and Trixie come into the anteroom. They are aging but still more or less elegantly dressed. Tiralira knocks at Osbert's door: no answer.

TIRALIRA. He doesn't answer, but we might as well wait here till lunch—and escape having to talk to Queenie—a darling woman, but a dreadful bore.

TRIXIE. He's been awfully busy lately. I think he's distinctly worried by the attacks in the conservative press. He's been taking a firmer stand. But it must be embarrassing for him to have to deal with the scandals of his father's government.

TIRALIRA. He's really more upset, I think, by Lucille's staying away so long in Phaiecia. He's beginning to be afraid that this time she's not coming back.

TRIXIE. I'm sure that he's really more comfortable living alone here in the Palace with Queenie. She spoils him, but I think he loves it.—Were you going to ask him about your modern museum?

TIRALIRA. Yes: I wanted to get an appropriation to buy up some Periwinkos and other things. There's a perfectly stunning nude that looks like the Central Power Plant!—I mean where you see all the pistons.

TRIXIE. I wanted to talk with him, too, about saving the old city churches. It's absurd that the government should encourage religion and then let the churches go to ruin. You know that lovely old transept at St. Kittywake-in-the-Bush is full of biri-biri birds' nests, and that fragile Frigidarius chapel that is just beside the Power Plant has so many windows broken that the smoke comes through and chokes the congregation—such as there are of them left.

Dr. Dish comes into the anteroom. He is venerable and well-dressed in black as if he occupied some distinguished post.

Dr. Dish. It would be well to save the churches, yes. They are the records of ancient belief. But I should deplore a return to religion—the emotional wrought-up states that the ritual and trappings provoke.

Trixie. Ah, you haven't the Faith, Doctor. If you had, you wouldn't speak so of our ritual!

Dr. Dish. I do not say that I am entirely devoid of faith, but we new Humanists do not admit that a decorous system of morals can be based on a supposed supernatural revelation.

Trixie. I don't deny the value of Humanism, but it is useless without the faith in revelation.

Dr. Dish. And I do not deny that Humanism may be supplemented by religion—if of not too expansive a kind. But one of the primary points that must be grasped is that Humanism is quite independent of religion and may dispense with it altogether.

Tiralira. What *is* Humanism, then, old boy?

Dr. Dish. Humanism is a moral system which has recently reached us from America.

Tiralira. Has Humanism anything in common

with those other American doctrines that have reached us from time to time: Christian Science, Constitutional Government, letting everybody vote for the Dictator?

DR. DISH. It has nothing in common with them. American Humanism is not democratic. It is, in fact, anti-democratic. We don't trust the common people, and don't want to do anything to benefit them because we don't think they deserve it. Humanism is mainly intended for persons of superior academic standing. I have found that I have always been a Humanist; for Humanism is not only opposed to democratic institutions: it is opposed to almost everything else. Its inflexible fortitude lies in its purely negative character. It is the conviction of the Humanist that virtue is exclusively a matter of refraining. Now, I knew that I had never been degraded by any of the turbulent passions. I had been refraining all my life. It was true that in my weaker moments, I had sometimes let my self-respect suffer by comparison with those irresponsible Bohemians whom the common man admires as poets, those reckless brutes he praises as heroes and those crackpots he follows as prophets. But now under Humanist discipline, I have learned how to patronize all these, and my spirit is perfectly at peace. I have nobody now to look up to, and I therefore experience no envy.

TRIXIE. You will never know perfect peace till you have eaten the bread of the Sacrament!

TIRALIRA. It's easy to eat the bread, old boy, but what I can't see for the life of me is how a fellow who used to joke as you did about the Seven Sacred Eggs of Saint Kittywake can swallow the Celestial Birth and the miraculous Resurrection of the Prophet.

TRIXIE. To have faith one must make oneself humble. When the Sacred Eggs seem absurd to us, it is because we have been deceived by our own foolish pride of reason. When we are humble enough, we comprehend these mysteries. There are, alas, so few people today who have risen to this height of humility!

TIRALIRA. You mean "sunk to this depth," don't you, old boy?—Well, I never make fun of the sincere believer; he has my entire respect. But for me it's enough to cherish beautiful things. It's enough for me to contribute my modicum of taste to the care of the Art Museum—to sit at home with my own few good pictures, with the delicious old furniture of the Megrims about me. I don't want to have to contemplate the ever so painful story of the Prophet's persecution and martyrdom—all the less if it should be true.

They go on talking while Osbert and Schenck come back into the Dictator's room.

OSBERT. I'm very much impressed, Mr. Schenck. What you've shown me is perfectly amazing.

SCHENCK. Of course, they're comparatively crude as yet, but I believe that in a few more years, with adequate personnel and equipment, I can turn out a human being that will make the present model obsolete.

OSBERT. Yes: they make one feel inferior in certain ways.—Their minds seem predominently technical.

SCHENCK. Technical: I suppose they are. I never sent them to school—all they know is what I've taught them. I'd set them to work on problems, and they'd carry things much further than I could. But you'd find they could make good at anything. It's just a question of training.

OSBERT. Of course. They share your own interests.—And they resemble you in other ways, too. You believe in slender people like yourself.

SCHENCK. That's only sound engineering. A maximum of energy and coördination to a minimum of bulk and weight. Of course, they're not so graceful-built as natural human beings, but if I could get a good anatomist to work on them, he'd be able to correct that.

OSBERT. How old are they?

SCHENCK. Ten to twelve.

OSBERT. Really? They seem mature.

SCHENCK. They are. I speed that up.

OSBERT. I believe I'd like to see them a little less prosaic.

SCHENCK. I admit that they're somewhat specialized. But too much imagination can be dangerous. You don't dispute the value of my work?

OSBERT. Oh, no: certainly not.—My dear Mr. Schenck, this whole experiment is undoubtedly enormously important and is going to make serious problems. I must take time to think about it. Come back in a week's time.

SCHENCK. OK, sir.

He goes out through the anteroom.

Tiralina now knocks at Osbert's door and Osbert opens it.

TIRALIRA. Have you a minute, old boy? I see you're alone. There's something I wanted to ask you.

Osbert admits him. Trixie, left alone, goes into the door to the Palace.

TIRALIRA. It's about the modern museum. I'm told that the whole thing could be done for not more than two million zukors.

OSBERT (*firmly*). Impossible, Tiralira, with thousands of people out of work. I'll have to put some of them on relief, and I can't spare a piffer on museums.

TIRALIRA. You admire modern art, I know, and—

OSBERT. And then, the new outlay for defense.

TIRALIRA (*disappointed and miffed*). I see.

OSBERT. Oh, by the way, Tiralira, I'd like that old paperweight that the Megrims used to have. It was always a favorite of mine. Danaë in the Golden Shower.

TIRALIRA. It's in the Museum now. It's the property of the State.

OSBERT. The Dictator is the State.

TIRALIRA. I don't need to tell you, old boy, that this is only a limited dictatorship, and I am Curator of Fine Arts. Anything that's connected with the arts has to have my approval.

OSBERT. The old Megrim furniture's not in the Museum. You've got it all in your own house.

TIRALIRA. It's too fragile to be exhibited.

OSBERT. I can always appoint another curator.

Queenie enters, a broad pink ribbon in her hand.

QUEENIE. I always knew there was something lacking, Berty. There's no ribbon on your waste-basket here! Don't you remember? Your mother always had one.

OSBERT. Oh, yes: thank you, my dear.

She ties it with a big bow. The Page knocks at the door of the anteroom, and Osbert opens it.

THE PAGE. A lady to see you, Your Excellency.

QUEENIE. Oh, do send word you're at lunch.

OSBERT. Who is it?

THE PAGE. She says you know her. She says to say it's Miss Emerald.

Emerald, not waiting for permission, comes into the anteroom, looking even more fierce and determined than in the sand-sifters' shack in Act I. She has with her a boy of twelve, with the military straightness of Emerald.

OSBERT. I'm afraid that I'll have to see her. You people go in to lunch—I'll join you.

QUEENIE. Please don't be too long, Berty.

She and Tiralira go out. Osbert, boldly smiling,
walks into the anteroom.

OSBERT. Well, Emerald, where did you come
from?

EMERALD. I've been here three months.

OSBERT. When I last heard of you, you were
in Leukopolis, the Leader of the Women's Legion.

EMERALD. I'm doing the same kind of work
here.

OSBERT. I didn't know we had a Women's
Legion.

EMERALD. I think there are a good many things
that you don't know about, Osbert. First of all,
that you have a son. Adalbert, this is your father.

Osbert and the boy are both embarrassed.

OSBERT. Why did you never tell me?

EMERALD. I saw no reason to. I went abroad at
the time of the Revolution. You got married; I
hadn't known I was pregnant. I'd got into trouble
for lèse majesté under the government of that
ruffian Rudolf, but I didn't want anything to do
with the reign of that bounder Bimbo. I made
myself a place in Leukopolis. The Phaiecians have
energy and discipline, and I've been worried when
I've looked over here and seen what difficulties
you were getting into with your sentimental half-
hearted liberalism. You must take a strong line with
your malcontents. Adalbert is proud of his father,
aren't you, Adalbert?

ADALBERT. I sure am: I've read everything about

you. All your books of poetry. They read you a
lot in Leukopolis. And I've read everything that's
written about you.

OSBERT. You mustn't believe all that stuff in the
papers.

ADALBERT. I don't believe the opposition papers.
I don't believe we're unprepared for war. I know
that you're just biding your time to strike.

OSBERT. You get that from the government
papers. Don't believe all you read in them either.

EMERALD. Don't shake his faith in you, Osbert.
(*To the boy*) Your father likes to pretend to be
cynical. (*To Osbert*) He's eager to take part in
the next war.

ADALBERT. We've got to show those Phaiecians
that they can't put tick-tacks on our consul's windows!

EMERALD. Let me talk to you privately, Osbert.
You go into the other room, Adalbert.

    *Adalbert goes into the reception room, where
he takes a cap pistol out of his pocket and amuses
himself by shooting at the objects in the room.*

EMERALD. You must acknowledge him, Osbert
—acknowledge him and have him succeed you.

OSBERT. An illegitimate son?

EMERALD. You haven't any other children.
Legitimatize him. Divorce Lucille. I can tell you
that Lucille has been sleeping with everybody of
any standing in Leukopolis, and you're the laugh-
ing-stock of Phaiecia.

OSBERT. Marry you?

EMERALD. You owe it to your dignity, and I shan't make any demands on you. You never did satisfy me. And now I'm a complete Amazon.

OSBERT. I don't want to fight the Phaiecians. I don't want to make this into a war state.

EMERALD. You'll have to sooner or later. The opposition's getting stronger, but I'm rallying the militant movement with the best of old Rudolf's Battleaxes and a youth group that's getting more and more belligerent. This is no time for liberal compromise.

OSBERT. Any birds and bears and morons among you old Battleaxes?

EMERALD. Don't be silly: they won't take discipline.

The Page knocks, and Osbert opens.

THE PAGE. Miss Queenie says please to come: The gardenia salad won't be crisp.

ACT IV

Osbert's sitting room in the Palace, furnished with the Megrim furniture, the clock with the allegory standing on the mantelpiece. Osbert, now six years older, is sitting in an armchair, fingering the Danaë paperweight. Trixie is sitting opposite.

OSBERT. Well, what brings you out in this bombing?

TRIXIE. It's poor old Tiralira. He's been miserable since you fired him.

An explosion and crash are heard. Trixie starts violently.

TRIXIE. Oh, there they go again!

OSBERT. I don't even wince any more. I know that if I happen to get killed, I'll have nothing more to worry about—and I think I'm due for a stroke, anyway. I've been having these dizzy fits.

TRIXIE. I'm sorry that you haven't *our* hope.

OSBERT. That I may be rewarded in the other world from which your Prophet descended? The legend about his birth is as silly as the legend of Danaë (*holding up the paperweight*): that Zeus came down in a shower of gold to impregnate her with the hero Perseus.

TRIXIE. That was an anticipation—a prophecy

228

in the form of a fable that the Divine would send
down to us a Savior.

OSBERT. To me, this is simply a creation of
beauty, a kind of clothing of a woman in splendor.
—But what were you saying about Tiralira?

TRIXIE. He's really in a pitiable state. He doesn't
get along with these creatures that all look like
Engineer-Biologist Schenck, and they won't give
him any kind of job.

OSBERT. Do you think that those creatures have
souls?

TRIXIE. That's a theological problem that hasn't
been settled yet.—But about Tiralira: he's starving
and he's living in wretched lodgings. You took the
best of his furniture away.

OSBERT. As you were saying, I don't share your
faith, so I don't try to live up to your ethos. Tiralira was always a damned rascal.

TRIXIE. Do you want to leave him to die?

OSBERT. We're all very likely to die.—I can't
take him in because he gives me the creeps. I can
send him a few rations. Don't eat them all up yourself.

TRIXIE. You do me a cruel injustice.

OSBERT (*wearily*). I'll see that you get some,
too.

He is seen giving an order on the house phone.

Emerald comes striding in, in military uniform.

EMERALD. Trixie, I see you're not doing your
bit.

TRIXIE. I *pray*.

EMERALD. You'd be better off praying in uniform. Of course you haven't got the guts for a soldier but you might make yourself useful at GHQ.

TRIXIE. I'm not sure I approve of this war.

OSBERT. Don't tell that to the Head of the Women's Legion!

EMERALD. I ought to be Minister of Defense, instead of that rubber-spined Fabius. If I had been, the war would have been won long ago! But you sit here on your fat liberal ass and try to sabotage our effort!

OSBERT (*to Trixie*). Go to the kitchen and they'll give you something.

TRIXIE. Thank you, Osbert. You do share our ethos in spite of what you say against it.

OSBERT. I'm damned if I share your ethos. It's an ethos that nobody could live up to. That's the last resort of you worshippers, to say that we're really one of you.

TRIXIE. Well, in any case, thank you, Osbert.

OSBERT. Uh-huh—as people say nowadays.— Tell Tiralira that if I see him again and he calls me "old boy" just once more, I'll be glad to let him die of starvation.

Trixie goes out.

OSBERT (*smiling wanly*). And as for my ass, Emerald, it's not half as fat as yours!

Emerald. You're a cad to insult me on account

of my sex—which I'm doing my best to suppress.

OSBERT. It's not true that I'm sabotaging the war effort. Did you hear my speech the other day?

EMERALD. It was drivel, it had no fire.

OSBERT. I'm afraid that I have to agree with you.

EMERALD. You compromiser! You coward!

OSBERT. I at least had the courage not to marry you.

EMERALD. Courage not to marry me! If you'd been a real man, you *would* have married me, and this would have been a real nation!

OSBERT. How is Adalbert doing with the Navy?

EMERALD. He needs more ships, and of course we haven't got them.

OSBERT. There's nothing for it now, I think, but to propose negotiations.

EMERALD. You mean to accept defeat, to back down before our enemies?

OSBERT. After all, we attacked them first.

EMERALD. To prevent their attacking us!

OSBERT. Lucille says that that isn't true: they didn't intend to attack us.

EMERALD. Lucille is a double spy. If you had had the spirit of a bumble-bee, you'd have sent her back to Phaiecia.

Lucille comes in, very chic.

LUCILLE. With all our boasted technological progress, I can't find a decent electric toothbrush, and my old one is all worn out.

Explosion and crash; Queenie enters.

EMERALD. You're worrying about your goddam toothbrush when civilization's at stake.

OSBERT. What do you mean by civilization?

EMERALD. Our wonderful country, of course—but not you, you poetasting milksop!—playing with your little paperweights!

QUEENIE. And now you must all come to dinner.
A louder and nearer explosion.

OSBERT. That sounded as if it hit the Palace.
The phone rings. He picks it up and listens.

OSBERT (*to the people in the room*). We were bombed by mistake by our own people.

QUEENIE. Oh, was anybody hurt?

OSBERT. Two killed. A few injured.

QUEENIE. Oh!
She starts for the door, and Osbert follows.

LUCILLE. I suppose this means no dinner!

EMERALD. Aren't you going to help?

LUCILLE. I can't bear to look at corpses. I wouldn't even go to see poor Count Klimny, who killed himself on my account.

Emerald gives her a scornful look and follows the others out.

EMERALD. It was perfectly deliberate no doubt—they want to get rid of their idiot non-Dictator.

OSBERT (*on his way to the door*). I'm still alive, my dear.

EMERALD. How long?

OSBERT.

"O Queen of air and darkness,
   I think 'tis truth you say,
And I shall die to-morrow;
   But you will die to-day."

*Another explosion close at hand. Osbert falls to
the floor, makes an attempt to get up but is help-
less.*

OSBERT (*indistinctly*). I'm half paralyzed. I can't
get up.

EMERALD. Ha!

*Queenie comes back and, seeing Osbert on the
floor, rushes to him.*

QUEENIE. Osbert!

OSBERT (*with painful effort*). I'm not—quite—
dead!

OPEN LETTER TO MIKE NICHOLS

1967

Dear Mike:

Apropos of your recent production of Lillian Hellman's *The Little Foxes*, I was going to write you a personal letter of suggestions for other American plays that I think it might be worthwhile to revive, a letter that you would hardly be in a position to act upon right away but that you might put away in your files. Now Walter Kerr's recent article in the theatrical section of the Sunday *New York Times* expresses a reaction so close to my own in connection with this performance that I think it may be a good idea to put these suggestions on public record in the hope that they may interest somebody.

The Little Foxes, says Mr. Kerr, "has left me filled with admiration and a kind of panic. Its one unmistakable message . . . is that we can have an American National Theater any time we want to. The materials are all there, ample and imperious and holding firm ground, on the stage of the Vivian Beaumont. My panic stems from the fear that we won't get it, that we won't hear what is being said, that, having come right to the edge of a discovery of our present powers, we will permit the decision to dissolve and the powers to scatter again as we always have through all of our long history." He goes on to speak of the excellence of the play, of

the cast and of your direction and to say that good
actors would not be lacking for "five or six other
companies just as good as the *Little Foxes* company . . . if anyone cared, or had the power, to call
them together. We *could* have five or six productions a year just as rich, just as resonant, just as
indigenous, just as serenely confident. . . ."

With all of this I agree, and I would add that
this production makes plain—what I have for a
long time suspected—that you are something of a
theatrical genius with an intelligence and imagination together with an ability to make them effective
which are excessively rare on Broadway. You may
remember that I used to see again and again—to a
point at which I had almost ceased to laugh at the
lines—your old show with Elaine May, in which
you two were able, alone, to take command of the
stage and get a response from an ordinary audience
to audacious partly improvised skits that exploited
a new sense of comedy. Since then, you seem to
have brought a magic touch to three comedies
which otherwise, I am told—I have only seen *The
Knack*—could hardly have been so successful; you
have managed, in the film you have made of *Who's
Afraid of Virginia Woolf?*, to stimulate to some
semblance of acting the attractive but—on her own
admission—the rather untalented Elizabeth Taylor;
and you have directed Barbara Harris in a delightful bill of three short musicals—one of them by
Jules Feiffer but the other two, rather surprisingly,

based on old stories by Mark Twain and Frank Stockton. The revival of *The Little Foxes* was, I understand, your own idea. You thought that here was an American play that ought to be a durable classic, and you and Mr. Saint Subber have given it a production which may well establish it as one.

Now, what I have long had a vision of and what I want to propose to you here is the eventual possibility of producing a cycle of American plays which might also become stage classics. I will give you a tentative list of these in more or less chronological order. They are not merely once popular plays whose former fame is still remembered—*Rip Van Winkle* would surely be impossible without Joseph Jefferson or *The Music Master* without David Warfield—but all plays that I have seen or read and that I think might still be made to work today.

Uncle Tom's Cabin. This is not ridiculous. The original scripts for *Uncle Tom's Cabin* were none of them very good, and by the time I saw it in my boyhood it had been turned into a kind of circus tent show, advertising two Topsies, who sang comic songs, two Uncle Toms, who did breakdowns, and, for a climax, Eliza crossing the ice, with the baying of bloodhounds offstage. But for the purposes of the Players' Club revival, in 1933, a special dramatization of *Uncle Tom* was made by Augustus Thomas, which, at a time when I had not read the novel, revealed for me for the first

time the real power of Mrs. Stowe's drama. It was
done by excellent actors: Otis Skinner was Uncle
Tom; Thomas Chalmers was Simon Legree; and
Topsy was done by Fay Bainter, one of the top
"comédiennes" of her period. All the characters
were played straight, including Topsy, who was
not merely a figure of fun but a genuine plantation
girl. Simon Legree was made, as he is in the novel,
not merely a whip-cracking overseer but a sadistic
New Englander with qualms, stranded on the Red
River with an unsuccessful plantation and an un-
happy mulatto mistress. This version has not been
published but it ought to be available. I predict
that, if properly directed and acted, it could not
but be a success. It would be interesting to see how
it would be received by the Black Power people,
who have derided as "Uncle Toms" the Negroes
that have succumbed to their humiliating situation
but have forgotten that Uncle Tom rebels and is
beaten to death for rebellion.

Fashion, or Life in New York, by Anna Cora
Mowatt, was first done in New York in 1845, and
travelled as far as London. It was revived by the
Provincetown Players in 1924, with such success
that it was taken uptown. The play was inter-
spersed with old songs—*Walking down Broadway,
Not for Joe, Call me pet names, dear, call me a
dove, etc.*—selected by Deems Taylor; and this
proved to be an excellent idea. I do not know
whether the comedy could stand by itself: it would

have to be presented, with some ironic accent, as a period piece. But it does have dramatic interest. At the Provincetown, it ran off amusingly and smoothly; and the speeches of Adam Trueman, the manly American farmer who denounces the New York swells, turned out to be quite rousing stage tirades.

I now come to what I regard as the two very best "Westerns" that I have seen in any medium. *The Girl of the Golden West* was produced in 1905 by Belasco. It was one of the plays that he wrote himself, and he boasted, no doubt correctly, that, from his early experience of California, he "knew the period of Forty-nine as I know my alphabet, and there are things in *The Girl of the Golden West* truer than many of the incidents in Bret Harte." It is a melodrama, but does not depend on expected melodramatic devices, and the atmosphere of the Polka Saloon and the Girl's cabin on Cloudy Mountain does create a compelling illusion even for a reader of the play, and without Belasco's realistic staging. About this staging, more later.

The next year, 1906, saw a Western of a different kind, *The Great Divide*, by William Vaughn Moody. Moody was a poet who had been to Harvard and at first wrote poetic dramas. But he had been born in Indiana and knew something of the Far West. *The Great Divide*, a sensation in its day, is not a melodrama, but a dramatic confrontation

of the American West with New England. The
situation created between, on the one hand, the
moral scruples and social conventions of Massa-
chusetts and, on the other, the lawless independence
and audacious speculation of Arizona brought out
a conflict of forces that had been shaking the ideals
of the East, and the play gave rise to much discus-
sion. The then shocking first act, in which a New
England girl in a lonely cabin saves herself from
being raped by three drunken invaders by offering
herself to the most prepossessing, who buys off one
of his companions and shoots the other, seems to
have stunned people in their seats, and what follows to have kept them petrified. I am aware that
this now sixty-year-old play would take a lot of
doing, and, since rereading it just now, I have been
haunted by an apprehension of the way in which
some of the scenes would sound if played by
Nichols and May. But I feel that *The Great Divide*
possesses enough artistic dignity to make it stand
up today. It has twice been made into a movie—
not, of course, that this proves anything except
that, like *Little Women* and *Huckleberry Finn*,
though never so popular as these, it may have the
makings of an American legend.

The middle of the first decade of the nineteen-
hundreds seems to have seen something in the nature of a belated fuller development on the part of
the more serious American theater. Bernard Shaw,
who had followed on the pretensions of Pinero and

the wit of Oscar Wilde and had behind him the authority of Ibsen, was now a predominating influence; *Man and Superman* was first produced in New York in 1905. Langston Mitchell's *The New York Idea* was performed in 1906, the same year as *The Great Divide*. Both Mitchell and Moody were literary men, and their plays were admirably written as well as well-constructed. *The New York Idea*, so far as I know, is the only really first-rate "comedy of manners"—*Fashion* does not quite qualify—ever written by an American dramatist. I saw it done, when I had not read it and had never seen it before, in a loft building on lower Fifth Avenue, without a regular stage, by a company of excellent actors who were otherwise out of work for the summer, and was astonished to find how amusing it was and how well it was still working under what would seem conditions extremely adverse to representing the monied milieu in which it is made to take place. The divorcing John and Cynthia Karslake are a smart Manhattan version of Congreve's Mirabell and Millamant, and they are more effective on the stage than their Restoration counterparts. Their love story, with its bristling hostilities, makes far more human appeal, and is brought to its tumultuous conclusion with as much wit and as little sentimentality.

This was also the heyday of Clyde Fitch, who was somewhat in the same line as Mitchell. But he wrote a great many plays and presents a particular problem. Which play of his could best be revived? Fitch did not have the gift, as Mitchell did in his single original play, of charging his social comedy with an effective emotional force. When Clyde Fitch is being funny with the special language and tone, the special preoccupations, of his period, he is natural and delightful. His American girls of the early nineteen-hundreds are amusing in the same sort of way as Scott Fitzgerald's flappers of the twenties. But when he tries to write serious scenes —though never so pompous as Pinero—he is theatrical in the bad old stilted way. His romantic historical plays—from *Beau Brummel*, written to order as a "vehicle" for Richard Mansfield, to *Captain Jinks of the Horse Marines*, which founded the reputation of Ethel Barrymore—would, I should think, be impossible today. Such a contemporary and rather ambitious comedy as *The Climbers* of 1901—which I never saw on the stage —is still readable for its social satire, but its straight dramatic scenes would be equally impossible. *The Truth*, of 1907, about a girl who is a compulsive liar, though coldly received in New York, became, on account, I suppose, of its pretensions to psychological interest, something of a European success. When I saw it revived in the spring of 1914—even with Ferdinand Gottschalk, that incomparably polished character actor who had been brought by Clyde Fitch from England and who was perfect for Fitch's comedies—it did not make much of an impression in competition with a current theater that was more psychologically advanced. Fitch's last and most ambitious play, *The City*, in which he was making an effort to get away from his lively young girls and to appeal to the then growing taste for the "unpleasant," with its violent climactic showdown in the second act between the drug addict and the corrupt politician—I used to pore, at fourteen, on the sinister posters—was produced in 1909, not long after Fitch's death. I read in the *Dictionary of American Biography* that "every seat was filled. The feeling was intense. By the end of the second act, the developing horror of impending catastrophe swept the audience into a demonstration seldom witnessed in a New York theater—a scene of hysterical confusion. Men were shouting, women fainted." I might well have been thrilled if I had seen it then; but I have only read it since, and it seems to me pathetic that Fitch should have founded his final hope to be taken seriously as a dramatist on such a contrivance of claptrap. Where Clyde Fitch is really strong is not in such melodramatic moralities, but in his playing with his world of early motor cars, Cunardars, big houses on Fifth Avenue, Americans in the Vatican Museum, Americans coming home with many trunks. If it is a question of a new production of a play of Clyde Fitch's, it ought to be some such comedy as *The Stubbornness of Geraldine* or *The Girl with the Green Eyes*. I remember, also, with pleasure a comedy called *Girls*, about what were then known as "bachelor girls" living uncomfortably in a New York apartment; but this, I find, has not been included in the four-volume selection of Fitch's plays published by Little, Brown.*

The problem of reviving Clyde Fitch brings me naturally back to Belasco. It was characteristic of the period in which they both triumphed that material objects were tremendously important. Edith Wharton's first published work was a treatise on interior decorating, and furniture, clothing and ornaments are always solidly described in her novels. (One is reminded that she and Clyde Fitch collaborated on a dramatization of her novel, *The House of Mirth*, which in its day was not a success and of which W. D. Howells is recorded by Mrs. Wharton as having said to her at the end of the first night, that "what the American public wanted was a tragedy with a happy ending." The script of this has not been published, but it is available in the Theatre Collection of the N. Y. Public Library and might be worth looking up in this connection.) It was the moment, *par excellence*, when Americans had begun to *buy things*, to be conscious of the acquisitions with which they had surrounded themselves. A revival of almost any play of Fitch's is almost unimaginable without his sets and his props. "He was often criticized," I learn from the *Dictionary of American Biography*, "for

* I now know that this was based on a German original, as were several of Fitch's plays, but he transposed it completely into terms of Manhattan.

his insistence upon small details; once a man sitting in front at a scenic rehearsal, exclaimed, as Fitch climbed down from the stage into the orchestra stalls, disgusted because some 'property' had not arrived: 'Why do you bother so much about such little things?' 'Because,' answered Fitch, 'I think they are *very important*; I believe in watching every bit of scenery, every action, every incidental blessed thing connected with the production. It is the "little things" that quickest show the lack of study and preparation.' " "Even in such a simple comedy as *Lover's Lane*," says the Introduction to his published plays, "during rehearsals, he spent hours fastening apples and pinning blossoms in the orchard scene." Belasco had the same preoccupation. He wanted to construct a detailed model of every indoor or outdoor scene that was required by a situation, and he loved collecting objects for this purpose. The sets of the Moscow Art Theater, which gave its first performance of Chekhov in 1898, also realized this ideal. In the case of an interior set, you were likely to see more than one room and to feel that the whole house existed. You came to feel that you were actually visiting an old-fashioned Russian family or the flophouse of Gorky's *Night's Lodging*, and trying to size up personalities and to make out what was going on.

This is a fashion, of course, that has passed. I first saw performances of Shakespeare in the days when the plays, always brutally cut, were continually interrupted to change the scenery from

"Venice. A Street" to "Belmont. A Room in Portia's House," or something of the kind; and I remember how delighted I was by a pioneer production of *The Tempest* at the New Theater in Columbus Circle, in which the piece was played through with no changes of scene. (The New Theater was an early attempt at serious repertory in New York, which, depending on the kind of rich subscribers who had been loyal to the Metropolitan but who did not care for serious plays any more than for serious opera, soon collapsed and fell back on *Old Heidelberg*, in which Gottschalk, Clyde Fitch now dead, did duty as a major domo.) I first saw Thornton Wilder's *Our Town* when it was being tried out in Boston, and its effectiveness was not impaired by its being performed with no background save the back of the stage itself, with its system of dingy pipes. In fact, the play could not have been done with a soda fountain, a small town interior, a funeral in the rain, etc. It might, perhaps, have been better without the pipes, but it had been writtten for a stage without scenery. I myself, when I write plays, usually revert to the older theater, and plan for a built-in Belasco set that will do for the whole play or will accommodate a few variations with a backdrop for a shallower stage.*

Now, Lillian Hellman, though much younger than I, seems also in this respect to derive from the

---

* The pieces in my *Five Plays* usually meet these requirements, but not those in the present volume.

Belasco period. *The Little Foxes*, though performed on a projected stage that was partly surrounded by the audience, was not only laid in 1900 but more or less conformed to the methods of that era. The elaborate permanent set might almost have been built by Belasco: the staircase at the back that dominated the room and played a part in the action; the decanters and trays and glasses and the old wooden box for the bonds were in harmony with the characters' costumes. And the play itself is a throwback to the model of an earlier decade. Miss Hellman says her critics complain that her plays are "well-constructed" and "melodramatic." I do not regard these as valid reproaches; and the very important respect in which *The Little Foxes* is not old-fashioned is that Miss Hellman does not only not feel under any obligation to write "a tragedy with a happy ending" but is not even aware of any necessity for calling her play either a tragedy or a comedy. (I am not sure, however, that the old impedimenta of realistic staging did not to some extent interfere with the success of her more recent and, for her, quite novel piece *My Mother and My Father and Me*, which I saw in its first stages in Boston and which seemed to me then badly hampered by the machinery of too many changes.) What I am getting at, Mike, however, is that anyone who can stage so successfully the early twentieth-century *Little Foxes* should have no difficulty whatever, if someone would provide the backing, in coping with *The Girl with the Green Eyes* or *The Girl of the Golden West. Uncle Tom* could be done without scenery, and probably ought to be. *Fashion* can perfectly be done with one of those conventionalized hardly-furnished interiors such as one used to see years ago in the Palais Royal farces in Paris and such as I suppose were made to serve for such drawing-room dramas as *Fashion*. But if you are going to revive Clyde Fitch, you will have to provide some equivalent for Fitch's paraphernalia.

I know that there is nothing so boring to the young as the theatrical memories of their elders. They don't believe that the actors and plays were so good as the old people say, the feeble attempts of the old people to impersonate the old actors are unconvincing, and in any case the young people don't want to hear about something they will never see. I find that I am getting close to indulging in this kind of thing, and you may be thankful that my narrowly American subject has not given me a chance to reminisce about the Abbey Theater's first production of *The Playboy of the Western World*, Vasily Kachalov in *An Enemy of the People*, or Lucien Guitry in the plays of Sacha. So farewell to you at this point and best wishes for more success in whatever you undertake. If God were not thought to be dead, I should beg Him to speed you, my boy, and to preserve you from the fleshpots of Hollywood, succumbing to which so many fine talents have foundered. (You should have seen Lionel Barrymore in this scene.)